DISCOVER FORENSICS

Enjoy "Discovering Forensics"!

Chen Yang

12 August 2018

DISCOVER FORENSICS:

How to Use Science for Investigations

By THE FORENSIC EXPERTS GROUP

Marshall Cavendish Editions

Published in 2018 by Marshall Cavendish Editions
An imprint of Marshall Cavendish International

A member of the Times Publishing Group

Other Marshall Cavendish Offices:
Marshall Cavendish Corporation. 99 White Plains Road, Tarrytown NY 10591-9001, USA • Marshall Cavendish International (Thailand) Co Ltd. 253 Asoke, 12th Flr, Sukhumvit 21 Road, Klongtoey Nua, Wattana, Bangkok 10110, Thailand • Marshall Cavendish (Malaysia) Sdn Bhd, Times Subang, Lot 46, Subang Hi-Tech Industrial Park, Batu Tiga, 40000 Shah Alam, Selangor Darul Ehsan, Malaysia

National Library Board, Singapore Cataloguing-in-Publication Data

Name(s): The Forensic Experts Group.
Title: Discover Forensics: How to use science for investigations / The Forensic Experts Group.
Description: Singapore : Marshall Cavendish Editions, [2018]
Identifier(s): OCN 1040026193 | ISBN 978-981-4779-28-9 (paperback)
Subject(s): LCSH: Forensic sciences—Juvenile literature. | Criminal investigation—Juvenile literature. | Evidence, Criminal—Juvenile literature.
Classification: DDC 363.25—dc23

Illustrations by Straight To Point Advertising

Printed in Singapore

Contents

the

WELCOME!

Hi there! Thank you for picking up this book!

Are you intrigued by how crimes can be solved using science? Do you want to find out how scientists examine and analyse different types of evidence?

If you do, **forensic science** is just the thing for you!

In this book, you will get to explore different disciplines in forensic science and find out how everyday objects can provide vital clues in the solving of cases. You will learn to debunk myths commonly depicted in TV programmes and immerse yourself in cases that made Singapore's headlines.

As you progress through the chapters in this book, learn about forensic document examination, damage analysis, trace evidence such as fibres and soil, corrosive liquids, and bloodstain pattern analysis. In the last chapter, we discuss the importance of ethics and integrity.

Armed with this knowledge, which builds on the science you learn in school, you will soon be able to answer the "who", "what", "where", "when" and "how" of crimes.

Remember — **every contact leaves a trace**!

Chapter 1

FORENSICS TO THE RESCUE

What is Forensic Science?

The word **forensic** [fuh-*ren*-sik] originates from the Latin word *forensics*, which means "in open court" or "public". Today, the term forensics, or forensic science, refers to the **application of science to laws**.

SCIENCE

LAW

Forensic scientists apply scientific methods and techniques to the examination of different types of evidence. The findings and conclusions from these examinations may be used to provide investigative leads and clues or aid in the administration of justice.

Key Principles in Forensic Science

The three key principles associated with forensic science are:

1. Principle of individuality
2. Principle of divisible matter
3. Principle of exchange

The principle of individuality states that "**No two objects are identical**" and that each object is unique. While two objects may seem similar at first glance, differences can be observed upon closer inspection or examination.

The principle of divisible matter states that "**Matter divides into smaller components when sufficient force is applied**".

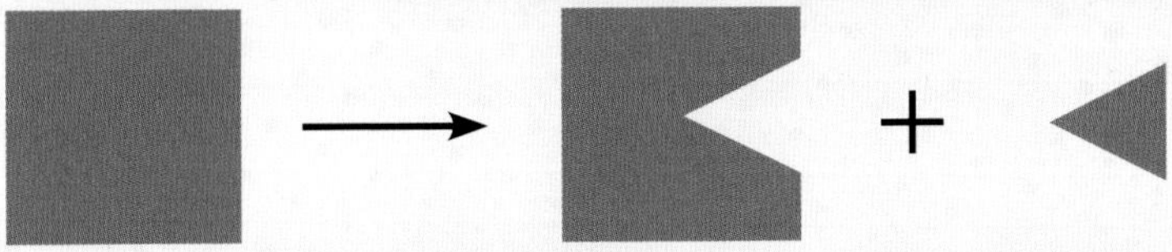

These two principles have a huge bearing on the individualisation or uniqueness of an object. This is particularly important in the examination of toolmarks and shoeprints, physical fitting and in linking or associating an object to a source.

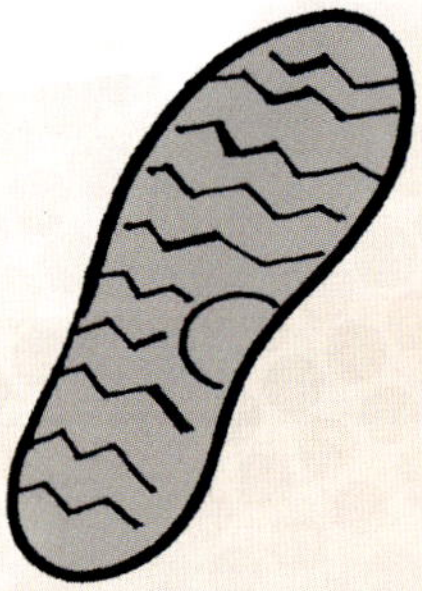

The third principle is more commonly known as Locard's Exchange Principle, which states that "**Every contact leaves a trace**".

When two objects come in contact, they will add something to or remove something from each other, usually unintentionally and sometimes unknowingly.

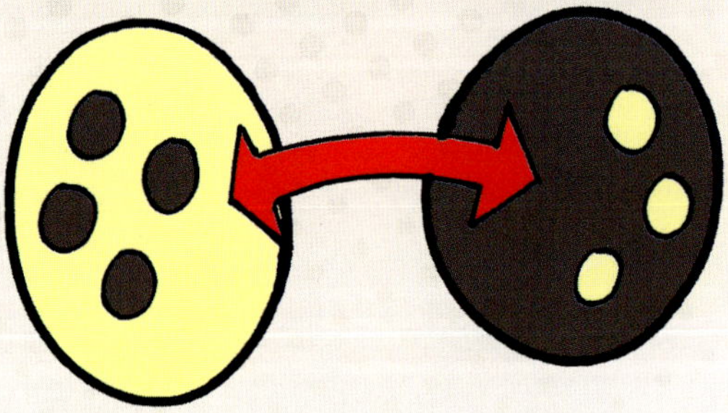

This principle provides the basis for transfer evidence such as DNA, fibres, paint, glass and soil. In a traffic collision where there is forceful contact, trace amounts of paint or glass may be transferred between the vehicles involved, or from the vehicle onto the victim. Similarly, in a fight where there is bodily contact between persons, fibres may be transferred from a person's clothing to another object/person.

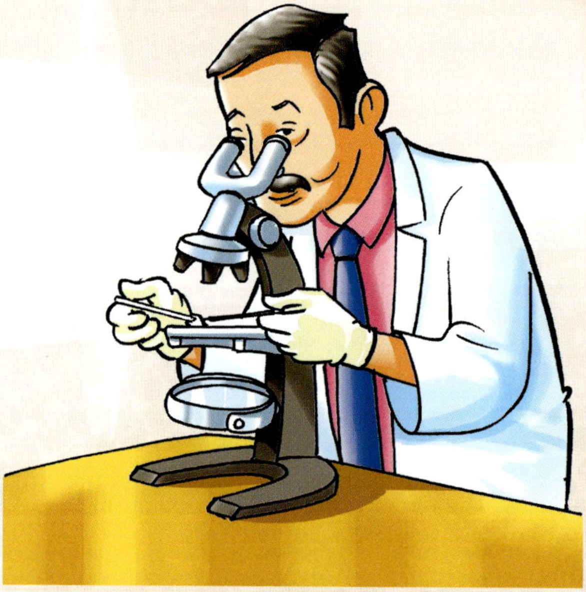

The pioneers of forensic science

Dr Edmond Locard (1877–1966), a French criminalist and a pioneer in the field of forensic science, is often regarded as the "Sherlock Holmes of France". He studied medicine and was interested in how science could be applied to the legal field. Hence, he went on to pursue a career in law.

Locard worked as a medical examiner in the French Secret Service during World War I and was able to determine the cause of death of soldiers and prisoners based on the bloodstains and damage on their uniforms.

He also made great contributions in the area of fingerprint identification but his greatest and most influential work was the development of **Locard's Exchange Principle**.

Another renowned scientist, Dr Paul L. Kirk, hailing from the USA, expanded on this principle in his book, *Crime Investigation* (1953):

> "Wherever [a person] steps, whatever he touches, whatever he leaves, even unconsciously, will serve as a silent witness against him.
>
> Not only his fingerprints or his footprints, but his hair, the fibres from his clothing, the glass he breaks, the tool mark he leaves, the paint he scratches, the blood or semen he deposits or collects.
>
> All of these and more bear mute witness against him. This is evidence that does not forget. It is not confused by the excitement of the moment. It is not absent because human witnesses are. It is factual evidence.
>
> Physical evidence cannot be wrong, it cannot perjure itself, and it cannot be wholly absent. Only its interpretation can err. Only human failure to find it, study and understand it can diminish its value."

Dr Locard put his principle to test when investigating several cases. One notable case occurred in 1912, when a Frenchwoman, Marie Latelle, was found dead in her parents' home. Her boyfriend, Emile Gourbin, was an initial suspect. However, he told the police that he had been playing cards with his friends on the fateful night and when the police questioned his friends, it appeared that Gourbin was telling the truth.

Locard, however, believed otherwise. Upon examination of Latelle's body, it was evident that she had been strangled to death. Taking a closer look at the scrapings from the underside of Gourbin's fingernails under a microscope, Locard found a pink dust-like material which appeared to be cosmetics.

Knowing that cosmetics were not mass manufactured during that time, Locard decided to dig a little deeper. Soon enough, he managed to find the chemist who had developed Latelle's custom-made powder and bingo, it matched the pink powder found under Gourbin's fingernails. Gourbin finally confessed to the murder and said that he had in fact tricked his friends into believing that he was with them at the time of the murder by adjusting the clock in the room to run ahead of time. With the conclusion of this case, Locard had once again proven that his Exchange Principle was spot on.

Recall your journey between two places today, e.g. from home to school. What are some types of materials you may have left behind or picked up along the way?

What types of evidence are there?

There are two types of evidence: **testimonial evidence** and **physical evidence.**

Testimonial evidence refers to statements given by a person or persons under oath.

Physical evidence refers to anything with shape and size. This means that everything around you can potentially be a piece of physical evidence. Even though the list may seem inexhaustible, forensic scientists have categorised the different types of physical evidence.

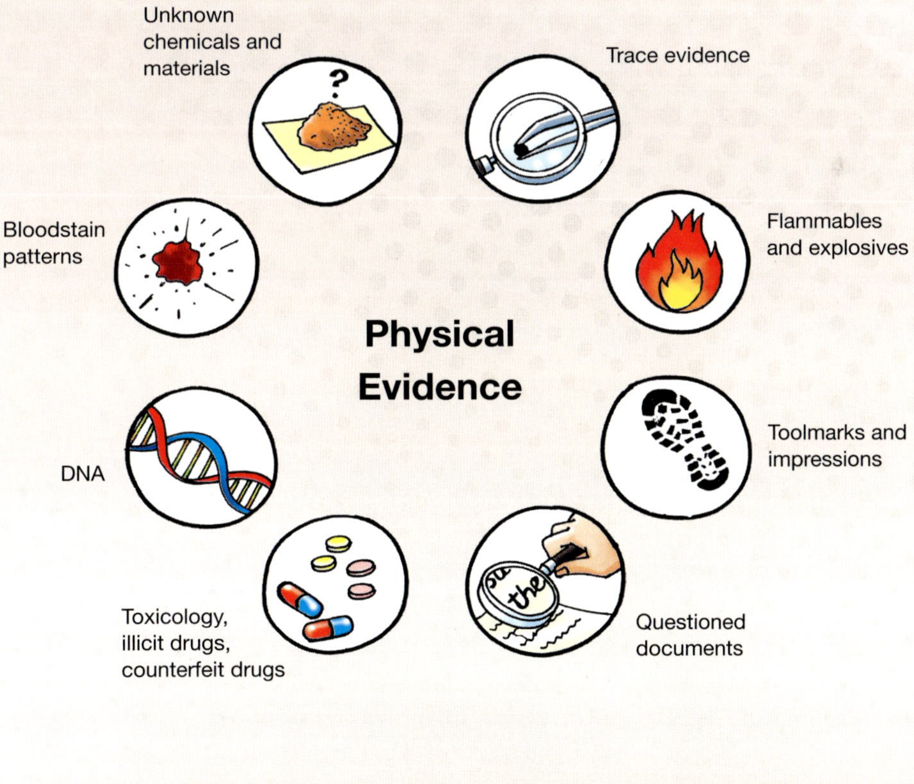

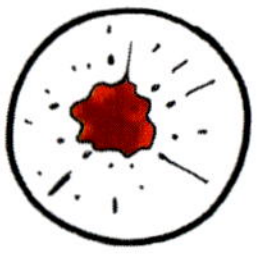

Bloodstain patterns

- The type of bloodstain pattern present at a scene can provide clues on the movement of persons, weapons used and events that occurred.

DNA

- One of the most well-known types of evidence, DNA can be extracted and analysed from hair roots, saliva, skin cells, tissues, semen and blood to identify the person(s).

Flammables and explosives

- In a fire or explosion, evidence such as fire debris, post-explosion materials or flammable[1] liquids may be collected.
- Analysis can help determine the identity of flammable liquids used, type of explosives used, or the origin of the fire/explosion.

Questioned documents

- Handwriting and signatures on disputed documents may be examined to determine authorship.
- Inks can also be analysed to link them to a particular source.

Toolmark and impression evidence

- Toolmark evidence include firearms, tools (e.g. a crowbar), and other items on which toolmarks are left.
- Forensic analysis of toolmarks may help determine if a bullet was fired from a particular firearm or if a particular tool was used in a break-in to damage a lock.

---

1. Flammable: Easily ignited and capable of burning quickly

- Impression or prints evidence include footprints, shoeprints and fingerprints, which are sometimes left at a crime scene or on items that the suspect touched.

Toxicology, illicit and counterfeit drugs

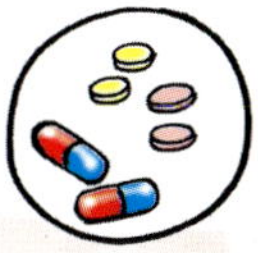

- Toxicology involves the study of adverse effects that drugs and chemicals have on humans and animals. Forensic toxicology thus plays an essential role in investigations involving poisoning, drug use or death, and suspected cases of doping.
- In the analysis of illicit[2] drugs, forensic scientists determine if the evidence contains controlled drugs that are stated in the Misuse of Drugs Act, and if so, quantitate the amount present. The quantity determined has a significant impact on the punishment imposed.
- Counterfeit[3] drugs are fake medicines. A forensic scientist can examine a suspected sample and through scientific analysis, determine if it is indeed a counterfeit or a genuine product.

Trace evidence

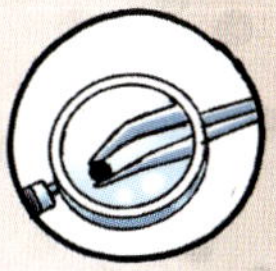

- Usually present in very small amounts and not readily visible to the naked eye.
- Easily transferred from one source to another.
- Examples include paint, fibres, soil and glass.
- Useful in providing associations or linkages between persons, objects and locations.

---

2. Illicit: Not permitted legally
3. Counterfeit: Made to look like the original of something, usually for illegal purposes

Unknown chemicals and materials

- May be encountered in cases of adulterated food, contaminated pharmaceutical products, or suspicious white powders.
- Analysis can help determine the identity of adulterants, contaminants or unknown substances.

Did You Know?

The field of forensic science is vast and the types of evidence that forensic scientists examine are not just limited to those above. Some of the other forensic disciplines include the following:

Forensic entomology is the scientific study of insects or other arthropods that are found on decomposing corpses. The stage of growth of the insects can provide an estimated time of death.

Cyber forensics involves investigation of information retrieved from digital devices such as computers and mobile phones.

Forensic pathology is the field where medical doctors perform autopsies on dead bodies to find out the cause of death.

Forensic accounting is the area where fraud, e.g. embezzlement of funds, is investigated. Forensic accountants usually apply their accounting and auditing skills to examine tax records, business invoices, financial statements, etc.

Find out More!

What other forensic disciplines can you think of?

What is it about physical evidence that makes it useful?

Firstly, physical evidence helps investigators **establish the key elements of a crime**: intent, conduct, concurrence, causation.

- **Intent**, also known as *mens rea* or "guilty mind", requires someone to have an intention to commit a crime, and to have the mental capacity to have intent.
- **Conduct** refers to actions taken by the accused, in the commission of the crime.
- **Concurrence** is often defined as the happening of two or more events at the same time.
- **Causation** refers to the intent and conduct of the accused that led to the crime.

Secondly, physical evidence is used **in crime scene reconstructions and forensic simulations** to answer the "who", "what", "when", "where", "why" and "how" of a crime or incident.

Did You Know?

Answering a "why" question in crime scene reconstruction does not refer to finding out the intent of a person associated with a crime or incident. Instead, forensic scientists seek to uncover the reason or explanation for an observed effect, such as "Why were there bloodstains observed at a particular height on the wall?"

The **identities of the persons** involved can also be established, and **linkages and associations** can be formed, connecting a suspect to a victim or a crime scene.

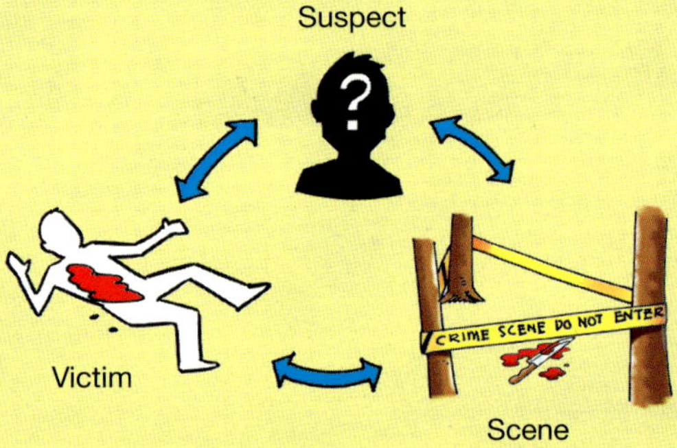

Physical evidence is also useful in **determining the reliability of testimony** from the victim or eye-witness, aiding in refuting or corroborating claims.

When confronted with physical evidence, suspects may make **admissions or confessions**. Conversely, physical evidence can also **exonerate the innocent** or prevent wrongful convictions.

Level Up! – True or False?

1. The more samples submitted for a case, the longer it takes to complete it.
2. DNA is the most important evidence in solving a crime.
3. You do not need a degree in forensic science to become a forensic scientist.
4. Results obtained from analyses are always absolute and definite.

Answers

1. **False.** The duration of analysis depends on the type of evidence, complexity of the case and scientific methods used. Therefore, a case with few samples may sometimes take longer to complete than a case with many samples. A case report can be completed within a day, or it may take weeks or even several months.

2. **False.** Other than DNA, which tells us the "who" of a case, there are several other types of evidence such as trace evidence, and damage and marks evidence, which can tell us the "what", "when", "where", "why" and "how" of a crime.

3. **True.** It is not necessary to have a degree in forensic science. Forensic science requires the application of knowledge from different domains of science such as chemistry, physics, biology and mathematics. The skills and knowledge needed are acquired through on-the-job training and attending specialised courses in specific forensic areas.

4. **False.** The results obtained from analysing evidence may not always provide an answer. Sometimes, inconclusive results may be obtained due to degradation of the evidence, insufficient evidence or wrongly collected evidence.

Chapter 2

Who Wrote This?

OP... The Writing on the Wall

Mr Chan, 55, came home late on Friday night to a ghastly sight! The front door and gate of his tenth-floor unit was splashed with red paint. His neighbour's unit also suffered the same treatment: "OP #10-1043" was written in red ink on the walls.

Mr Chan immediately contacted the Police who launched an investigation. Within days, they apprehended the culprits. It turned out that his neighbour had borrowed heavily from loan sharks and was unable to pay up. The loan sharks then dispatched runners to vandalise his unit. The unfortunate Mr Chan had been collateral damage.

How do you think the police were able to identify the suspects?

Did You Know?

- **OP:** Owe Money Pay Money
- **Loan shark:** Unlicensed moneylender
- **Runner:** Someone who acts on behalf of an unlicensed moneylender and whose job may involve defacing/causing damage to the exterior surroundings of the borrower's flat.
- **Collateral damage:** A term generally used for damage inflicted on an unintended target.

Handwriting Examination

Albert Sherman Osborn was the founder of the American Society of Questioned Document Examiners (ASQDE) and considered by many to be the father of the science of questioned document examination. He was also instrumental in the forensic investigation into many of the biggest cases in his day, including the Lindbergh Baby Case. His book *Questioned Documents* is regarded by document examiners all over the world as the seminal text in the field.

Albert Sherman Osborn
(1858–1946)

Did You Know?

The **Lindbergh Baby Case** was regarded by many as the "Trial of the Century". On 1 March 1932, the 20-month-old son of world-famous aviator Charles Lindbergh was kidnapped from his home. A handwritten ransom note asking for $50,000 was found. Subsequently, more ransom notes were received and after negotiations, the ransom money was dropped off for the kidnapper. Unfortunately, the baby was never returned and his remains were found on 12 May 1932. Investigations continued and from the recovered evidence, forensic document examiners determined that the ransom notes were written by the same person. The forensic evidence coupled with investigations by law enforcement eventually led to a suspect, Bruno Richard Hauptmann. Bruno Hauptmann was convicted and executed in 1936.

What is Handwriting Examination?

Handwriting examination is the **determination of authorship** through the comparison of **questioned writing** with **specimen writing**. The basis of handwriting examination is built on the following scientific principles:

Uniqueness — No two persons write exactly alike. Just like how your fingerprints are unique, no one writes exactly the same as you.

Natural Variation — No one writes exactly the same way twice. Try writing the same word three times, and have a look at them. Are they exactly the same? Human beings are not like machines that can perform repeated movements with the same precision and accuracy each time. Hence, our writing tends to differ even when writing the same word, resulting in natural variation.

(Repeated) Characteristics — While there may be slight differences in our writing due to natural variation, there are characteristics within a person's handwriting that are consistent and repeated.

Did You Know?

These are some terms used in handwriting examination:

Determination of authorship: The identification or elimination of a writer, i.e. did this person write or not write this writing?

Questioned writing: Writing that is disputed or has come into question.

Specimen writing: Undisputed or known writing of the writer that can be used for comparison with the questioned writing.

What do forensic scientists look for?

To determine who wrote the questioned handwriting, forensic scientists examine characteristics such as the construction and spacing of letters, and a person's writing pressure and skill. For example, consider the letter "t". It may be written with either the horizontal or vertical stroke first.

Forensic scientists do not rely on just one or two obvious similarities or differences in the handwriting characteristics. A conclusion must be based on a combination of characteristics through a thorough and detailed comparison between the questioned and specimen writings.

In some cases, the forensic scientist may encounter disguised handwriting where an individual deliberately changes his handwriting such that it has obvious visual disparities with his usual handwriting, in a bid to conceal his identity.

Graphology is *not* forensic handwriting examination. Find out why!

Writing Instruments

Writing instruments have always been indispensable in the task of handwriting. The figure below shows the milestones in their history. Which of these writing instruments are you familiar with?

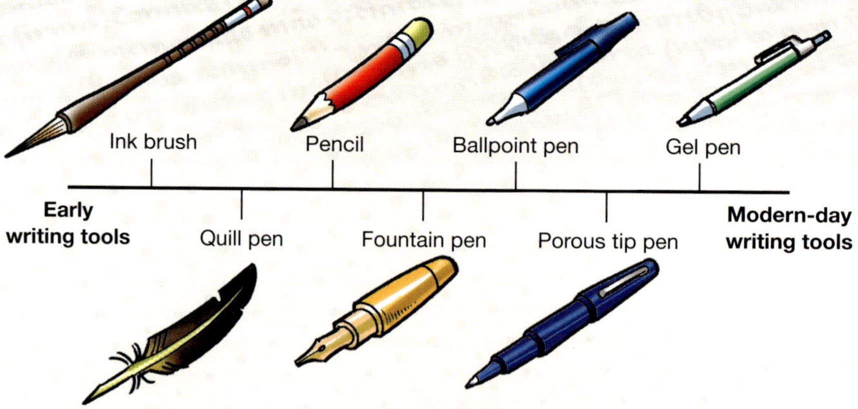

Did You Know?

The creation of the ballpoint pen is often credited to the Hungarian journalist László Bíró. However, the concept for the ballpoint pen was patented as early as 1888 by American John Loud. Unfortunately for Loud, his idea did not lead to any viable commercialisation. It was only in 1938 that Bíró first patented the pen that would eventually gain widespread popularity such that it is still in use today.

Close-up of a ballpoint pen tip

What led to the ballpoint pen's commercial success was its oil-based ink. The ink was able to dry quickly without creating smudges and could also be used at high altitudes, unlike fountain pens, which tend to leak due to pressure differences.

In a ballpoint pen tip, a ball sits in a socket and dispenses ink through its rotation as the pen is drawn across the page. Gravitational forces transfer ink from the ink reservoir onto the paper. Different ballpoint dimensions result in different line widths.

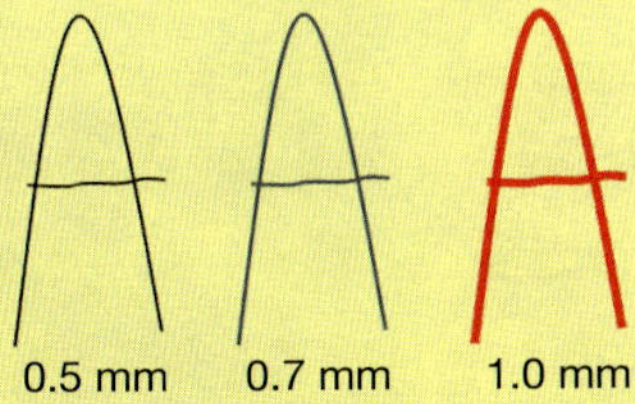

Do you have a favourite pen? What is its line width?

Ink

Inks are liquids or pastes that contain pigments or dyes.

Development of Ink through the Ages

2500 BC

The ancient Egyptians and the Chinese both developed ink around 2500 BC. They used fine particles of carbon called lampblack for the colourant, and gums or glues as the bonding agent.

5th–15th Century

By the Middle Ages, iron gall ink was the main ink used. The black or brown-black ink was made of iron salts and tannic acid and was used for both writing and drawing.

Johannes Gutenberg invented an oil-based printing ink in the 15th century.

20th Century

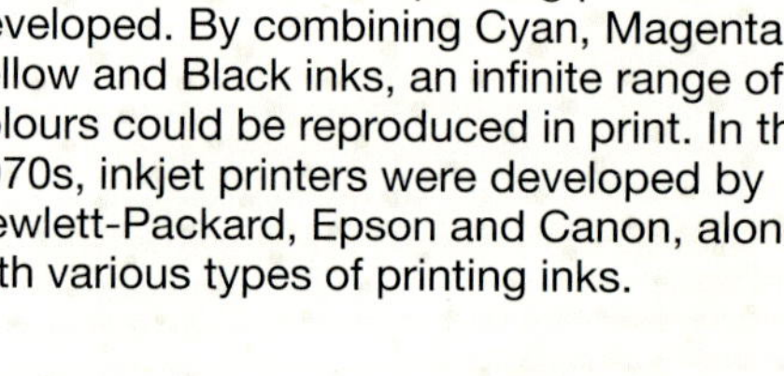

The CMYK four-colour printing process was developed. By combining Cyan, Magenta, Yellow and Black inks, an infinite range of colours could be reproduced in print. In the 1970s, inkjet printers were developed by Hewlett-Packard, Epson and Canon, along with various types of printing inks.

Analysis of Writing Inks

Physical Methods – Visual and Microscopic Examination

When you look at a piece of writing, consider the following.

- What colour is the pen ink?
- What type of writing instrument was used?

Ballpoint Pen

Characteristic pasty appearance, due to the thick consistency of the ink

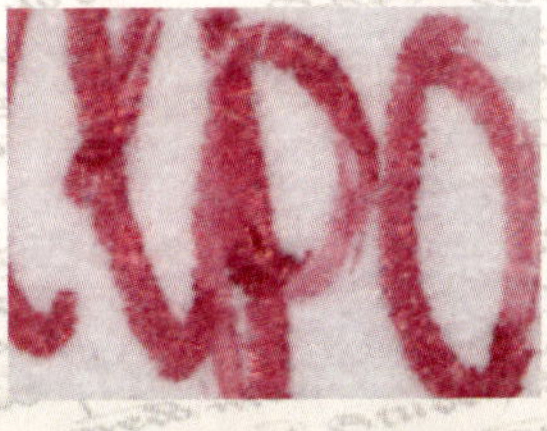

Gel Pen

Presence of a lightly inked centre portion in the ink line, resulting in a characteristic track mark

Fibre-tipped Marker

Writing line is solid and uniform, though individual fibres may fray and produce fine lines alongside the main ink line

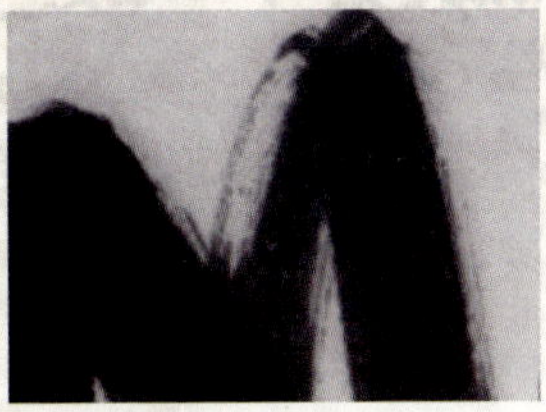

Are components of the ink used in ballpoint and gel pens similar or different?

Chemical Methods — Thin-Layer Chromatography

Chromatography is a technique that separates a mixture (e.g. ink) into its respective components. This technique was first developed in 1903 by Russian botanist Mikhail Tsvet, who used filter paper to extract plant pigments such as carotene and chlorophyll from leaves.

Forensic scientists often use thin-layer chromatography (TLC) to separate inks. The ink sample is spotted (i.e. deposited as a spot) onto a TLC plate and placed in a tank containing a mixture of solvents. As the solvent mixture travels up the TLC plate, the ink components are separated into different coloured spots.

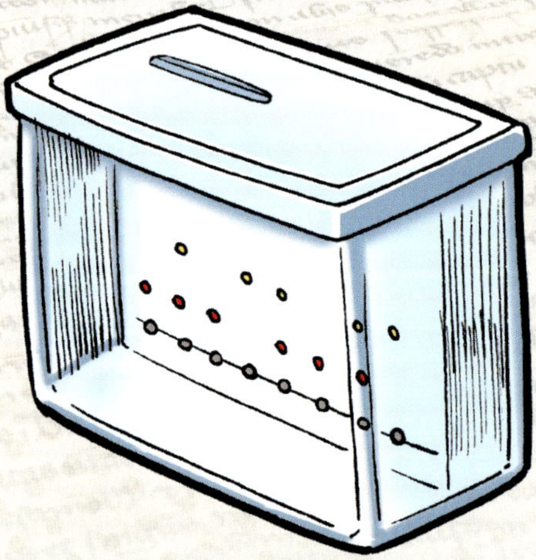

Besides being used as ink for writing or drawing, dyes and pigments are also used in the automotive industry as paint coating for vehicles, or in the textile industry to impart colour to fabrics. Can you think of some other uses for dyes and pigments?

Did You Know?

How did people obtain dyes and pigments in ancient times?

Plants

Yellow dye was extracted from saffron, turmeric, and weld.

Insects

Red or scarlet dye came from an Arabian insect from the genus *Kermes*.

Sea creatures

Black was made from the ink that octopuses produce, blue-black from squid's ink, and brown from cuttlefish.

Tyrian purple was obtained from the mucus of the *Murex* sea snail. Due to the difficulty of extracting this dye, the colour became highly prized and was often only used by royalty.

From the Vaults – Stories from Singapore's Past

The Fall of Barings Bank

In 1995, Barings Bank, one of the oldest banks in Britain, collapsed. It was due to the huge losses incurred by its 28-year-old Singapore-based trader, Nick Leeson. Leeson racked up a huge debt for the bank, amounting to billions, after incurring losses from unauthorised trading. When further discrepancies were uncovered by the bank and linked to him, Leeson quickly left for Malaysia before fleeing to Germany.

Back in Singapore, officers from the Commercial Affairs Department (CAD) were able to recover documents from Leeson's office and handed them to forensic scientists for examination. The handwriting expert provided evidence that Leeson had falsified documents to cheat Barings Bank. The expert had compared the signatures from different letters, and found each signature to be exactly the same, indicating they were copies made from one signature.

The findings of the handwriting expert played a part in detaining and extraditing Nick Leeson from Frankfurt Airport to Singapore to stand trial for his crimes. He was eventually charged with three counts of forgery and eight counts of cheating, and was sentenced to six and a half years in prison.

To prevent similar incidents from happening, changes to the Futures Trading Act were made, which allowed the Monetary Authority of Singapore (MAS) to closely monitor the activities of traders selling futures.

Level Up! – Collect Your Handwriting

Print a copy of this page from our website:

www.forensicexperts.com.sg/discover-forensics/whowrotethis

Write the following passage in the empty box below and send it to us!

Dear Jennifer,

How are you?

It is a public holiday today in Singapore as we are celebrating our National Day! Our National Day falls on 9th August and I always look forward to watching the live broadcast of the parade on television.

When is your country's National Day and how do you celebrate it?

Excited to hear from you and I hope to visit you quite soon!

Your Pen-pal
Zak

P.S. You can also contact me at +65 29137804 if you wish to text or call me!

The above passage was written by ________________, age _____.

By sending the above handwritten passage to us, you have given us permission to use your handwriting as part of our scientific research. Thank you for your contribution!

Chapter 3
WAS IT A CUT OR A TEAR?

During an assault or a murder, the clothing of the parties involved may be damaged. This damage may be caused by objects such as knives and cutters, or due to forceful interactions between people. A forensic scientist conducts **damage analysis** in order to gather information from the damaged items.

From the examination of the damage on an object, e.g. clothing, the forensic scientist can deduce:

- If the damage was recent or old
- The nature of the damage, whether it is a **cut**, a **tear** or normal **wear and tear** due to repeated use or aging of the material

- The action that caused the damage, such as **cuts made by sharp objects** e.g. box-cutter, knife, scissors, shard of glass, or **tears caused by force**

What is the difference between a cut and a tear?

A cut is usually produced by an object with a sharp edge, like a pair of scissors or a knife, and leaves behind neat edges on the material. Different sharp-edged objects can produce different types of cuts and these cuts can be differentiated based on their physical appearance.

A tear, in comparison, results from the material being pulled apart with force, resulting in irregular edges.

Other than sharp objects and large forces, other causes of damage to fabrics include friction, heat, chemicals and electricity.

- **How will a tear resulting from a force differ from that caused by normal wear and tear?**
- **Tools such as knives and box-cutters are known as single-bladed tools, while scissors are known as double-bladed tools. Can you tell why?**

Level Up! – Find my match

Know your knives!

Match each knife in Column 1 to its correct name (Column 2) and to its uses (Column 3):

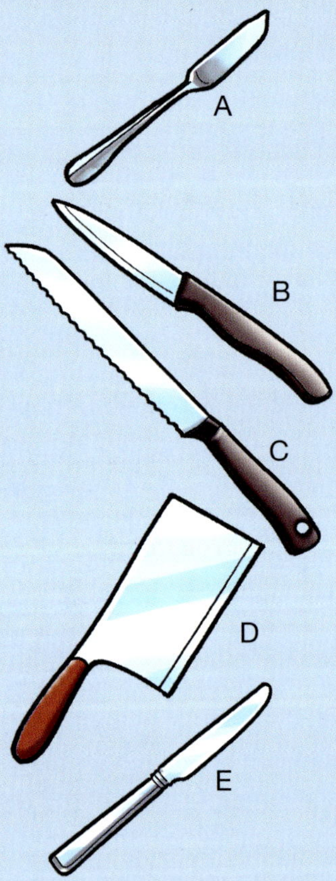

Butter knife	• Non-serrated knife used to serve butter from a dish.
Cleaver	• Knife with a notched tip used to separate and pick up bones to be placed on a plate.
Paring knife	• Serrated knife used to cut soft bread without crushing it.
Bread knife	• Large kitchen knife used to hack through bones.
Fish knife	• Small knife ideal for peeling or for intricate work.

WARNING: DO NOT play with sharp objects. They can cause serious injuries!

Did You Know?

- In traffic collisions, the high impact between a vehicle and a pedestrian may cause some fibres from the pedestrian's clothing to fuse with the coat of paint on the vehicle.
- Strong acids and alkalis can cause chemical "burns" to fabrics.
- When a person is struck by lightning, the large amount of electricity can cause clothing to shred, melt or burn.

Let's Investigate!

A 25-year-old man dressed in sports attire was found lying motionless on a soccer field by his friends. They called for an ambulance but he was pronounced dead at the scene.

The group of friends had been playing soccer that evening when it started to rain and thunder was heard. A decision was made to stop the game and they left the field. After some time, several of them realised that one of their team-mates was not with them. They went back to the field to look for him and found him on the ground.

The deceased's socks and spiked shoes were sent to your laboratory for analysis. During your examination, you made the following observations and findings. What do you think likely happened?

Observation and Findings

Each of the deceased's shoes had two metal pins on the sole, near the toe region. Holes were observed on the inner soles of the shoes, just above the position of the metal pins.

A hole was found at the side of each sock, at the position of the large toe. The edges of these holes had melted material adhering to them. The melted material was found to be from the shoe lining.

What likely happened?

The damage observed suggested that a bolt of lightning was likely to have struck the man, travelling through his body and out via the shoes to the ground. The passage of the lightning current created intense heat, resulting in holes with melted material around the edges. As the current was conducted to the ground through the metal pins in his shoes, the parts of his socks and shoes around the metal pins showed severe damage.

Damage to materials

Damage in fabrics depends on the construction and type of fabric, the type of tool and the action causing the damage. Fabrics are constructed or made from natural fibres or synthetic fibres. Synthetic fibres are made from polymeric materials. Polymeric materials or plastics, as they are commonly known, are also used in the mass manufacture of various household products.

Besides damage to fabrics, forensic scientists are also involved in examining damage on other types of polymeric materials such as the insulating layer on electrical cables, rubber tubings, synthetic ropes and cordages, safety harnesses and slings.

Think about the adhesive tape you use to hold or fasten items together. Are you able to tell if the tape ends were torn or cut using a pair of scissors?

Level Up! – Find My Match

Can you match the different items to the materials used to make them?

A: Rope

B: Plastic bags

C: Non-stick pan

D: Bulletproof vest

Kevlar® **Polyethylene** **Hemp** **Teflon®**

A. Hemp B. Polyethylene C. Teflon® D. Kevlar®

Did You Know?

Researchers are constantly trying to create new polymers that possess desirable properties such as self-healing ability, high tensile strength and high thermal stability. Kevlar® and Teflon® are examples of polymers that possess such desirable properties.

Kevlar® (Poly-paraphenylene terephthalamide) was first developed by a chemist, Stephanie Kwolek, in 1965 and is five times stronger than steel! Kevlar has a wide range of applications. Apart from protective gear, it is also used in the manufacture of racing canoes and tyres.

Teflon® (Polytetrafluoroethylene) possesses excellent thermal stability, does not ignite easily and is waterproof. These properties make it a suitable material for non-stick cookware.

From the Vaults – Reverse Bungee Cord Snaps: Accident or Sabotage?

In May 2006, while preparing to be launched into the air, one of the cords of Clarke Quay's G-MAX Reverse Bungy snapped.

Forensic scientists were tasked to examine the damaged bungee cord and determine if it was an accident or an act of sabotage.

From the analysis, it was found that the damage to the bundle of rubber strands of the bungee cord was not due to cuts by a sharp

instrument or object. Instead, the fracture of the rubber strands in the cord was due to aging, tension and fatigue, indicating that the damage was due to wear and tear.

Did You Know?

The interior of a bungee cord consists of thousands of elastic strands, imparting both **elasticity** and **tensile strength** to the cord. These strands are bound together by a braided exterior sheath made from either nylon, polyester or polypropylene.

Elasticity: The tendency of a material to revert to its original form (shape) when a force applied to it is removed.

Tensile strength: The amount of pulling force a material can withstand without being permanently damaged.

Chapter 4

TRACKING CRIMINALS WITH FIBRE EVIDENCE

Fibre evidence falls under the category of **trace evidence**. Trace evidence refers to small and microscopic amounts of material which are not visible to the naked eye. Apart from fibres, other examples of trace evidence include paint, soil, glass and gunshot residue.

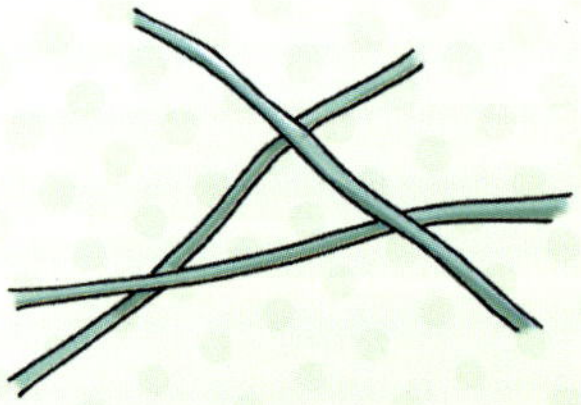

Fibre

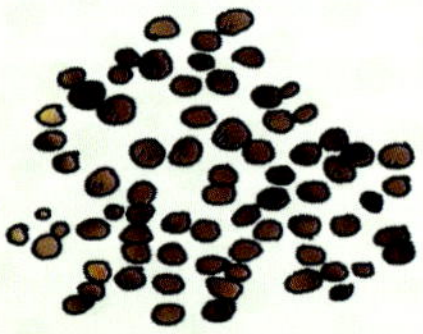

Soil

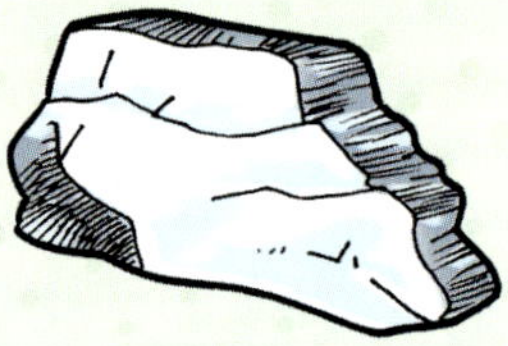

Glass

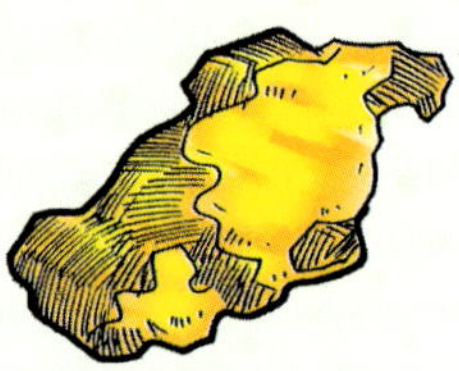

Paint

Trace evidence is usually **transferred through physical contact** during the commission of a crime or the occurrence of an incident. This transfer can occur between persons, objects or places. For example, paint material on the tip of a crowbar used in a house break-in, glass fragments on a pedestrian involved in a traffic accident or gunshot residue on a shooter's hands and clothes.

Microscopic gunshot residue left on the hand(s) and clothing of the person who discharged a firearm.

Paint fragments on the tip of a crowbar used in a break-in.

Fibres, Fibres Everywhere!

We are constantly surrounded by fibres — the fibres on our bedsheets, the towel we use after a shower, the clothes, socks and shoes we wear, the bag we carry, the car seat we just sat on! These fibres are all easily transferred between sources when contact is made.

Take a Look Around!

How many sources of fibres can you spot?

Did You Know?

The cross-section of fibres may have interesting shapes!

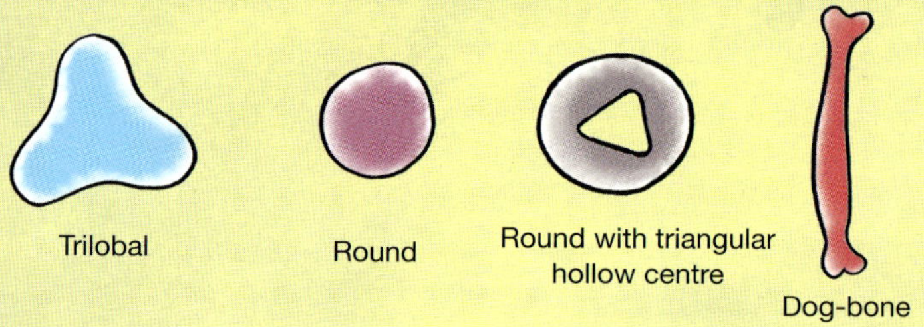

What is a Fibre?

A fibre is the smallest unit of a textile material or fabric and is typically an elongated material with its length many times greater than its diameter. Fibres are typically spun into lengths of yarn before they are **woven** or **knitted** into a piece of fabric.

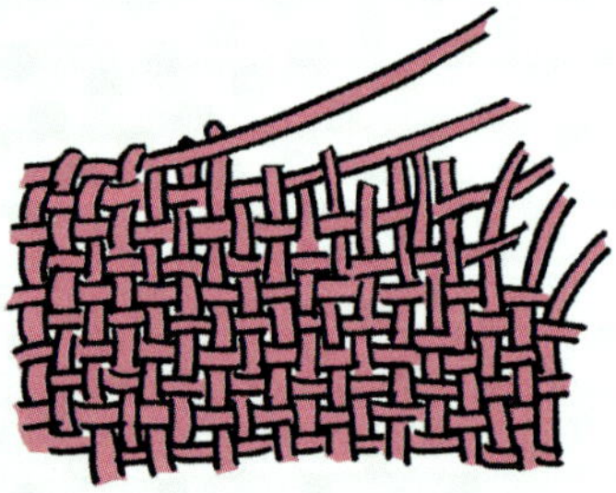

Woven material

Peek into Your Closet!

Look through the different articles of clothing that you have in your closet. Are they made of woven or knitted fabrics? You'll be able to find out using a magnifying glass!

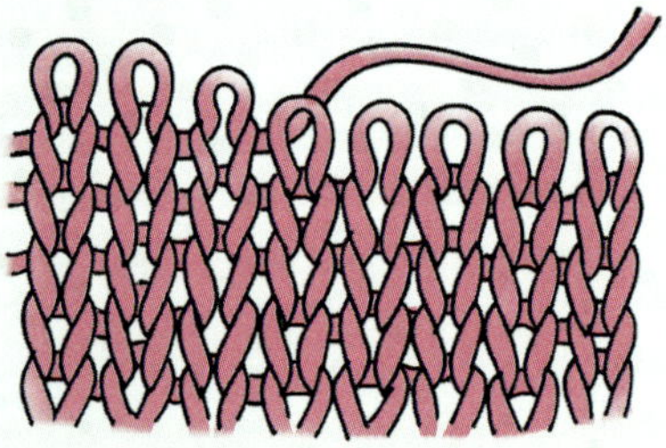

Knitted material

Types of Fibres

Fibres

- **Natural**
  - **Plant**
    - Leaf (e.g. sisal, abaca)
    - Seed or Fruit (e.g. cotton, kapok)
    - Bast (e.g. flax, hemp, jute)
  - **Animal**
    - Wool
    - Silk
  - **Mineral**
    - Asbestos
- **Synthetic/Man-made**
  - Polyester
  - Polyamide (nylon)
  - Polyethylene
  - Polyurethane

Did You Know?

- Bast fibres are fibres from the phloem of plant stems.
- Synthetic/man-made fibres are made with a chemical process known as **polymerisation,** where small molecules join together to form long chains.

- Another type of man-made fibres are **regenerated fibres**, e.g. rayon. These fibres are made by dissolving the cellulose component of plant fibres in chemicals. Following that, they are re-formed to create fibres with desired characteristics.

How is fibre evidence useful?

Every contact leaves a trace (Locard's Exchange Principle)
There are two means of transfer or exchange of evidence: direct transfer and indirect transfer. Indirect transfer occurs, for example, when evidence from someone ends up on an item without them having touched it.

Establish contact between persons
In assault cases, a violent struggle between two persons would involve forceful contact between two bodies, causing an exchange of fibres between them.

Establish contact between a person and an object
In a traffic accident, the impact between a moving vehicle and pedestrian can cause fibres from the pedestrian's clothing to fuse onto the exterior of the vehicle. In addition, fabric imprints may be observed on the vehicle.

In kidnapping cases, there may also be an exchange of fibres between the victim and the car seat.

Establish contact between a person and a scene
In a burglary, the suspect may leave behind fibres from his clothing or gloves on a broken window, or on surfaces he may have touched during the break-in. Similarly, the suspect would have likely brought away fibres from the objects he had come in contact with at the scene.

Let's Investigate!

A brown duffel bag suspected of containing controlled drugs was seized by customs officers. The packages in the bag were examined and found to contain heroin. Two men who were seen carrying this bag were arrested, but both of them denied ownership of the bag.

Subsequent checks of the flat where both the men lived revealed another 12 similarly packed packages of drugs.

Investigators want to establish if there was contact between the two suspects and the bag.

As a forensic scientist, what would you examine in order to form associations between the suspects and the bag?

Examination Findings

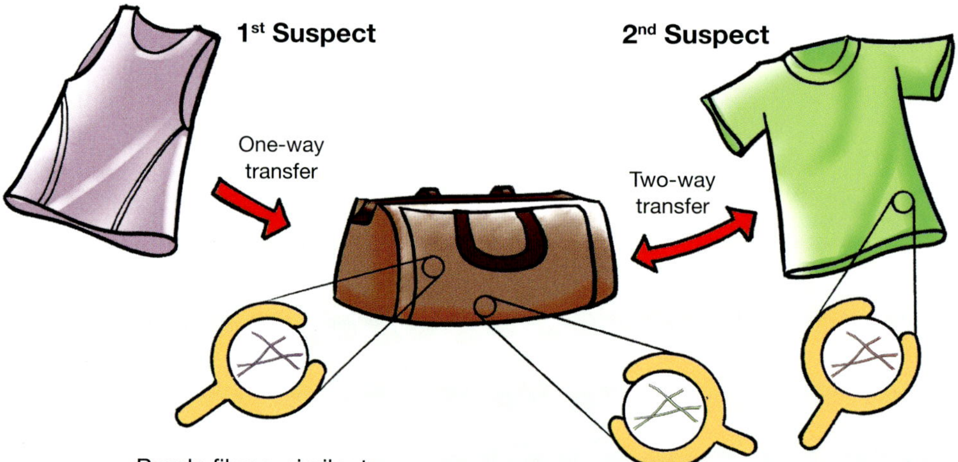

Purple fibres, similar to the fibres of the singlet worn by one of the men, were found on the brown duffel bag.

Green fibres, similar to the fibres of the green T-shirt worn by the second man, were found on the bag.

Brown fibres, similar to the fibres of the bag, were found on the green T-shirt.

Association was found between the two suspects and the bag containing drugs.

Did You Know?

Singapore has very strict drug laws. Depending on the amount of controlled drugs carried, drug traffickers can be hanged. For example, according to the **Second Schedule of the Misuse of Drugs Act (CAP 185)**, a person caught trafficking more than 250 grammes of methamphetamine will face the death penalty.

A Hairy Situation

A trained and experienced forensic scientist is able to tell a lot by looking at the characteristics a sample of hair, from its colour and cross-sectional shape to its microscopic structural features.

Parts of a strand of hair

Hair comprises three main layers — the cuticle, cortex and medulla.

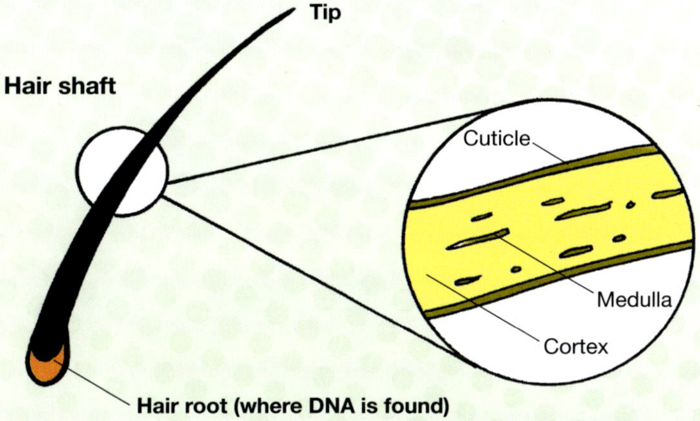

- The **cuticle** is the outer layer of the hair shaft and consists of scales that overlap.
- The **cortex** is the middle portion of the hair shaft and contains most of the pigments that give hair its colour.
- The **medulla** is a group of cells found in the centre of the hair. In some people, the medulla is absent, whereas in others, the medulla may be broken or it may be continuous.

Hair-nalyse This!

Look at the hairs on different parts of your body. Are they similar in appearance and texture?

Interesting Facts about Hair

Straight vs Curly

Hair of different textures has different cross-sections.

Natural vs Coloured

When hair is dyed, colour pigments deposit within the cuticle or cortex. When hair is bleached, chemicals are used to destroy the natural hair pigments.

Why does hair turn grey or white?

Melanin is responsible for the colour in our hair. When the amount of melanin in our hair decreases, especially when we age, it turns grey or white.

A perm is a hairstyle resulting from treatment that sets the hair in curls or waves. What happens when hair is permed?

Each strand of hair is held together by disulphide bonds. During the perming process, these bonds undergo a reduction-oxidation reaction, where they are first broken and then formed again after the hair has been placed on rollers to create curls.

Human hair or animal hair?

Forensic scientists can identify if a sample of hair is from a human or an animal by looking at it under a microscope. This is because hair from humans and different animals possess distinctive characteristics such as length, colour and the appearance of the medulla and the scales on the cuticle.

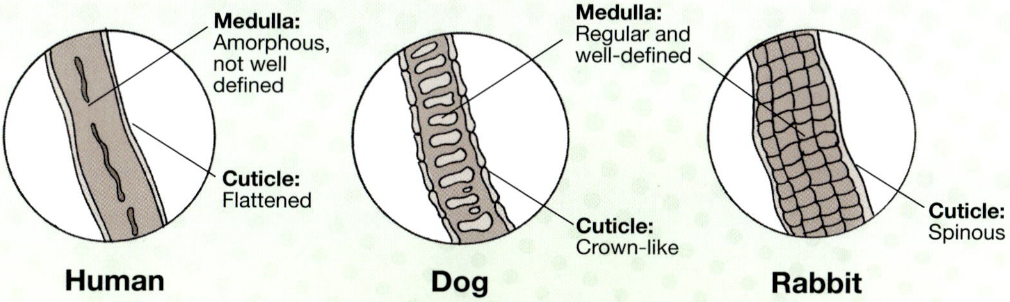

$$\text{Medullary index} = \frac{\textit{Diameter of medulla}}{\textit{Total diameter of hair shaft}}$$

Humans → less than 1/3

Animals → more than 1/3

True Crime

Springfield, Massachusetts, USA

On the night of 30 October 1985, a burglar broke into a 78-year-old woman's house and raped her. George Perrot, 17, was arrested and subsequently sentenced to life imprisonment based on a single strand of hair found on the victim's bedsheet. The single strand of hair was the only physical evidence placing Perrot at the scene — no semen or blood was found and thus no DNA test could be done.

During the trial, an FBI agent named Wayne Oakes testified as an expert witness. He claimed that he was an expert in hair and textile fibres and that because the head or pubic hairs of individuals were distinctive, he could distinguish hair samples belonging to different persons. He also claimed that in his 10 years of experience, it was extremely rare that he was unable to tell apart the hair samples from two individuals. He convinced the court, based on the microscopic features he observed, that the strand of hair belonged to Perrot.

Perrot was sentenced to life imprisonment even though the victim testified that Perrot did not look like her attacker, whom she said had short hair and was clean-shaven. Perrot, on the other hand, had long wavy hair, a moustache and a goatee. She also failed to identify him as her assailant in a police line-up.

It was not until 30 years later in 2016 that a Superior Court judge ordered a new trial to be heard, as the use of microscopic hair analysis to identify a person was deemed to be flawed. Perrot was eventually exonerated in 2017.

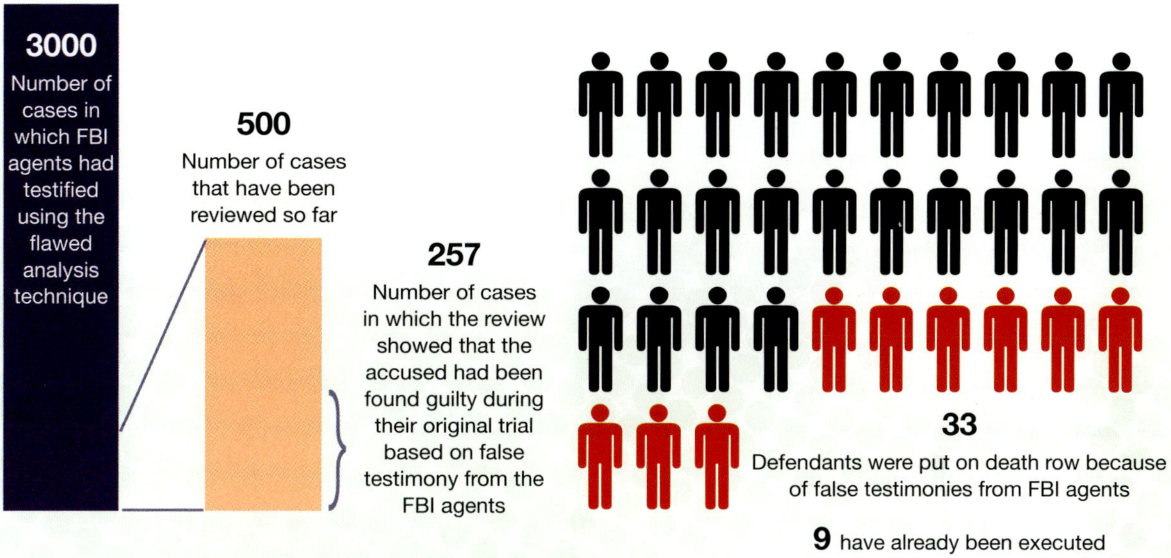

Lesson learnt

Forensic scientists must recognise the strengths and limitations of each scientific technique used in the analysis of evidence. They must also be committed to presenting conclusions that are reliable and rigorously supported by and based solely on the evidence.

Did You Know?

The **Innocence Project** was started in a bid to exonerate those who have been wrongfully convicted, such as in the case of George Perrot, by using DNA testing. Read more about the Innocence Project in the chapter on *Forensic Scandals*.

Chapter 5

TRACKING CRIMINALS WITH SOIL EVIDENCE

From the Vaults -- Crimes from Singapore's Past

On the morning of 20 October 2008, Mr Wang and his friends were jogging along Lorong Sesuai, opposite the old Bukit Timah Fire Station, when they were hit by an overpowering stench of decay.

What they initially thought to be a dead animal turned out to be the decomposed body of a woman in a beige T-shirt and a pair of dark blue trousers; her head was covered with a piece of cloth.

What happened?

On 16 October 2008, Mr Rosli Yassin met up with Ms Choo Xue Ying regarding some business. Both of them were in the car that Choo was driving when she stopped her car along Lorong Sesuai.

They were discussing the money which Rosli claimed Choo owed him. During their argument in the car, Rosli started hitting Choo on the head and face many times.

Rosli then suggested that both of them discuss the matter outside the car and they got out.

When Choo said that she wanted to call the police, Rosli snatched her phone, then punched and kicked hit her repeatedly until she fell.

Rosli carried her body to the bottom of a slope in a forested area and left her there where she eventually succumbed to her head injuries.

As Rosli was driving off from Lorong Sesuai in Choo's car, he hit a tree. He subsequently abandoned the car at Jalan Kubor and fled with her laptop and handbag.

How do you think soil evidence was used in this case?

What is soil?

Soil is a complex mixture of the following:

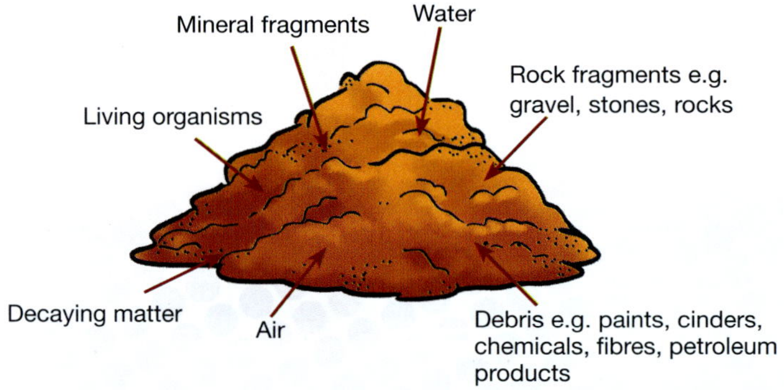

The four major types of soil particles are:

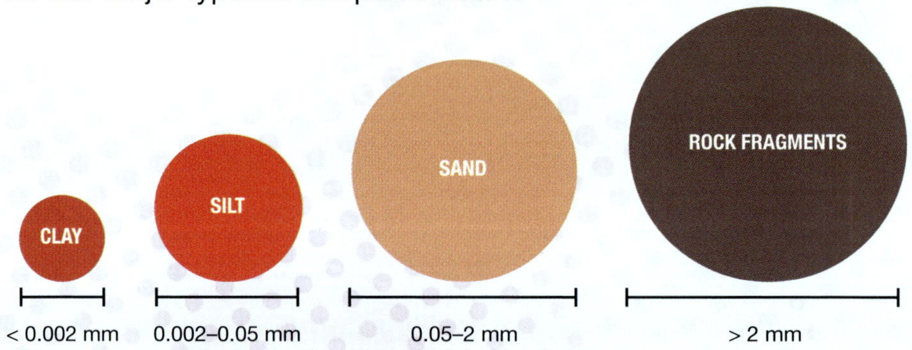

The importance of sand, silt and clay in soil

Sand: Allows water and air to flow through soil.

Silt: Holds on to water, which plants can take up and utilise.

Clay: Holds on to nutrients such as magnesium, potassium and calcium, which plants absorb to help them grow.

Let's Dig Deeper

Collect soil from different locations. Examine each sample using a magnifying glass. How similar or different are they, in terms of colour, size and particle types?

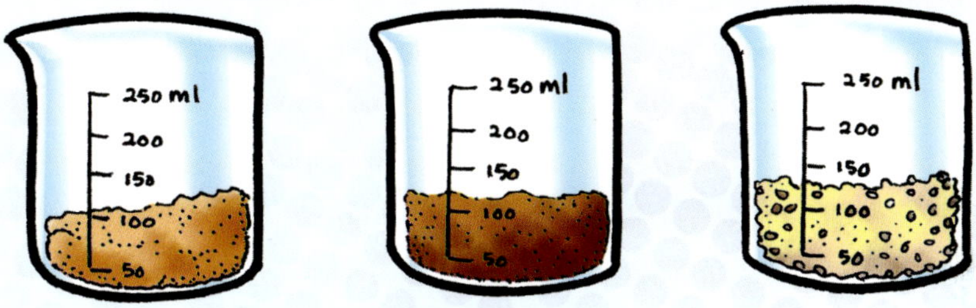

Field Garden Roadside

Organic and Inorganic compounds in soil

Soil consists of a mixture of organic and inorganic compounds. The organic compounds originate from the decomposition of matter and substances made by the living organisms in the soil. Inorganic compounds originate from the weathering of various rock types.

Organic compounds

Contain mainly carbon (C) and hydrogen (H).

Inorganic compounds

Contain mainly silicates of aluminium (Al), iron (Fe), calcium (Ca), potassium (K), sodium (Na) and magnesium (Mg).

Soil Density

The density of soil samples is examined using a **density gradient column**. Why? This is because soil particles are too tiny for their density to be calculated using their mass and volume.

A density gradient column consists of layers of liquids, each with a different density.

Because soil is a mixture of particles with different densities, the different soil particles will suspend in a liquid with a similar density.

Did You Know?

- The top layer of soil is usually trapped in the soles of shoes or on clothing during a crime.
- Only a small amount of soil is needed for examination – about one to two teaspoons.
- Before construction begins on a plot of land, soil testing is done to determine the type, suitability, quality and strength of soil.
- In countries such as the USA, soils from different geographical locations differ in their compositions. The uniqueness of soil from different locations can help investigators pinpoint a region or location where a crime was committed.
- Forensic scientists use a colour chart such as the **Munsell Soil Chart** to assign a colour to a soil sample.

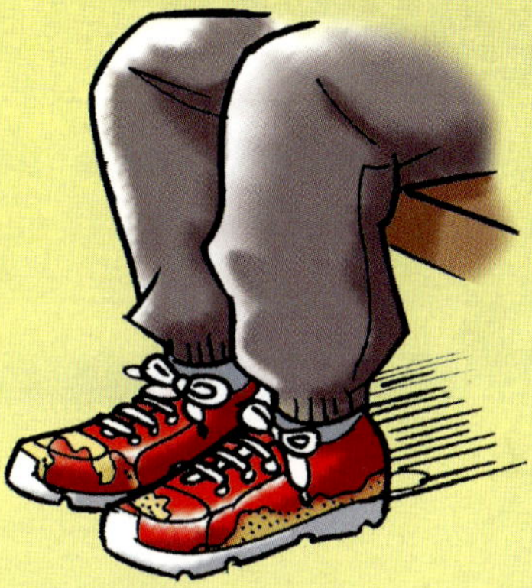

Let's Investigate!

A gruesome discovery

At about 9:15 am on 16 June 2005, a cleaner discovered a brown cardboard box along the bank of Kallang River. When he tried to pick it up, the box broke apart. The contents that fell out of the box looked like fresh meat wrapped in newspapers and a green plastic bag. Unfortunately, it was not — it was the lower torso and thigh of a woman!

On the same day, a second carton containing an upper torso, with arms and hands attached, was found on the opposite bank of the river.

An island-wide search was conducted and two days later, a decomposed head and a pair of lower limbs were found at an incinerator plant in Tuas.

The victim was identified as 22-year-old Liu Hong Mei, a Chinese national working as a production operator.

The suspect, Leong Siew Chor, 50, claimed that both he and Liu had decided to commit suicide together but he backed out of their pact.

However, the truth of the gruesome murder soon came to light.

What really happened

On 13 June 2005, Leong had stolen Liu's ATM card and used it to withdraw money from her account to purchase some items.

The next day, Liu made a police report, and said that she could review the CCTV footage to try and identify the culprit.

In order to silence Liu, Leong strangled her in his home in Geylang on 15 June. He dismembered her body into seven parts and concealed them using newspapers, plastic bags and cardboard boxes.

He then discarded Liu's body parts, clothing and belongings at different parts of the island. Even though her head, upper and lower torsos were recovered, Liu's feet were never found.

Items seized from Leong's flat

These items were examined by forensic scientists and the findings linked Leong to the dismembering and discarding of the victim.

What do you think they were used for?

Question

Knowing the locations the accused had travelled to when disposing of the body parts of the victim, what other types of evidence can we gather?

(Hint: Think about his footwear!)

Answer

We can look at the soles of the footwear that the accused was wearing. Why?

The grooves in the soles of our footwear are excellent places for collecting sand or soil particles. The next time you walk across a field or along a beach, look at the soles of your footwear and you'll find soil or sand particles lodged there.

Examining the soles of the footwear that the accused was wearing could provide investigators with clues to the places he had been to.

If he had been near a river bank or coastal area: Sandy particles containing micro-shells may be trapped in the soles of his footwear. If these particles match soil particles retrieved from the crime scene, it would link the accused to the scene.

If he had been to a forested area: There might be a mixture of dried leaves and soil particles trapped in the soles of his footwear. The composition and density of the soil particles can be examined to help investigators narrow down the possible places he had been to or link the accused to a particular location.

Chapter 6 OUCH, IT HURTS!

From the Vaults – Stories from Singapore's Past

"Hot Seat" on the MRT

On 2 May 2013, a 24-year-old nurse sat down on the MRT without realising that the seat was wet. The liquid stung her skin and left her with burns that required treatment at the hospital. What was on the seat? Was it perhaps some sort of acid, and how did it get there?

Laboratory analysis found that the liquid was likely to be sodium hydroxide, which is a strong alkali found in many household cleaning products. More investigations were conducted, and it turned out that a previous passenger had placed a leaking bottle of concentrated dishwashing detergent on the seat and had failed to clean up the spill or to notify the authorities.

The passenger was charged with causing grievous hurt through a negligent act and was eventually fined $4,500. The maximum penalty for the offence is a jail term of two years and a fine of $5,000.

In Singapore, there is a legal act that governs the unlawful possession or use of corrosive and explosive substances. This act is known as the Corrosive and Explosive Substances and Offensive Weapons Act. Find out what the penalties are. Are there similar legal acts in other countries?

Acids and Alkalis

Acids

- Have a sour taste
- React with some metals to produce hydrogen gas
- React with carbonates and bicarbonates such as baking soda to produce carbon dioxide gas
- Neutralise alkalis
- pH less than 7
- Can be commonly found — some of them around you and some of them in you!
  - » Acetic acid, which is found in vinegar and has a distinctive pungent smell
  - » Hydrochloric acid (HCl) that forms the stomach acid used to digest food

Alkalis

- Have a bitter taste
- Are slippery to the touch
- Neutralise acids
- pH more than 7
- Present in our surroundings:
  - » Sodium carbonate, present in the detergent you use to clean your dishes
  - » Magnesium or aluminium hydroxide, present in antacids. Antacids are used to treat or relieve heartburn, which is the regurgitation of stomach acid into the oesophagus.

Please do not attempt to taste acids or alkalis!

Acid + Alkali → ?

When an acid reacts with an alkali, neutralisation occurs, producing a salt, water and heat.

When an alkali is added to an acid, the pH of the solution increases towards 7, which is neutral.

Did You Know?

The most well-known salt is the salt we find in the food we consume daily. It is known by many names: common salt, table salt, sodium chloride (chemical name) or by its chemical formula, NaCl.

How do you test for hydrogen gas and carbon dioxide gas?

pH and its Measurement

pH (potential of hydrogen) is a measure of the acidity or alkalinity of an aqueous solution on a scale of 0 to 14.

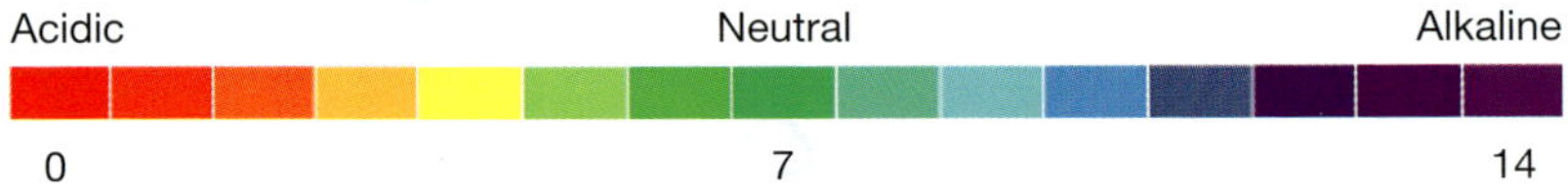

pH can be measured using an indicator. A pH indicator is usually a chemical compound that undergoes a colour change over a range of pH. Some of the commonly used indicators are phenolphthalein and methyl red.

Commercial pH indicator strips

Litmus paper

Red litmus paper turns blue when in contact with alkalis.
Blue litmus paper turns red when in contact with acids.

Universal indicator strips provide a closer approximate of a solution's pH as they cover a range from 0 to 14. To use a universal indicator strip, place a drop of the test solution onto the indicator strip, observe the colour change and match it to the corresponding colour on the pH colour chart. If a more accurate pH reading is required, a pH meter should be used.

Level Up! – Slot Me In

Can you place these household products on the pH scale?

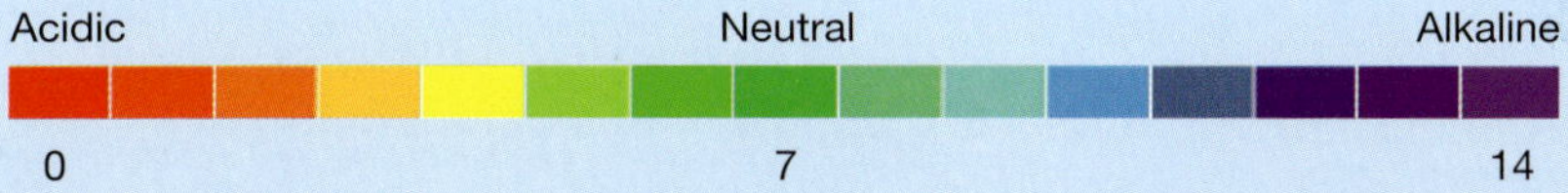

What do you think is the pH in your stomach?
How about in your small intestine?

Let's Investigate – Secret Message

Now you see it, now you don't

Organic acids such as citric acid in lemon juice can be used to send secret messages. At room temperature, these acids are colourless and can be used to write your message. Upon safe delivery, the intended recipient can use heat from a lamp or a steam iron to reveal the hidden message. This is because heat causes the acid to oxidise and turn compounds in the paper brown, thereby making the message visible.

Go ahead, send your friend a secret message

Just remember to scribble something on the paper with a regular pen or pencil as a decoy.

Are strong acids and alkalis found around us?

One may think that strong acids and alkalis are present only in laboratories or factories. However, some household cleaning products can be sources of chemical burns, especially if they are used inappropriately or without proper protective gear.

The following are some household cleaning products that you may be familiar with:

- Bleach
- Drain cleaner
- Laundry detergent
- Toilet cleaner

Always read product labels to find out whether they are acids or alkalis, and how they should be used.

Many of these household cleaning products require dilution before use. For example, the instructions provided may require you to add one capful of the cleaning agent to half a pail of water.

Dilution is also carried out in chemistry laboratories. However, such dilutions are carried out accurately using **volumetric glassware**.

Which laboratory apparatus allows you to measure volume most accurately?

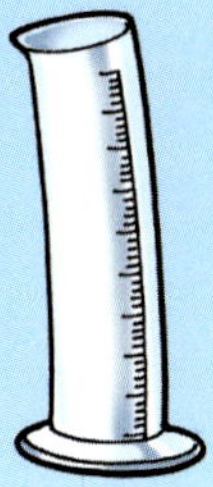

Measuring cylinder

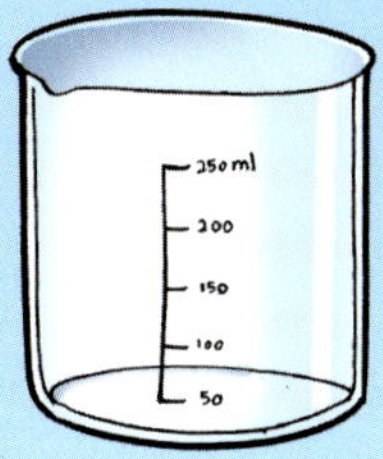

Beaker

Volumetric flask

Serial Dilution in the Laboratory

How would you go about diluting a solution by 10 times or 100 times? We would perform **serial dilution**. This is a stepwise procedure where a solution is first diluted, and the diluted solution is then further diluted to obtain the required concentration.

To perform a 10-times dilution of apple juice concentrate

Pipette 1 mL of the apple concentrate into a 10 mL volumetric flask. Top up the flask with water to make a 10 mL solution.

To calculate the concentration of the diluted juice:

$$(C_{\text{Apple concentrate}})\,(V_{\text{Apple concentrate}}) = (C_{\text{Diluted juice}})\,(V_{\text{Diluted juice}})$$

$$(C_{\text{Apple concentrate}})\,(1\text{ mL}) = (C_{\text{Diluted juice}})\,(10\text{ mL})$$

$$(C_{\text{Diluted juice}}) = \frac{1\text{ mL}}{10\text{ mL}}\,(C_{\text{Apple concentrate}})$$

Formula

$C_1V_1 = C_2V_2$

Legend

C = Concentration

V = Volume

The concentration of the diluted apple juice is now 1/10 of its initial concentration.

To perform a 100-times dilution

Take 1 mL of the above diluted solution and repeat the above process to obtain a 100-times diluted solution.

What are the advantages of performing serial dilution, as compared to performing a 100 times dilution directly?

From the Vaults – Stories from Singapore's Past

In 1999, a three-month-old baby was subjected to an acid attack by a domestic helper working for his family. The domestic helper fed sulphuric acid into the baby's mouth and the attack badly damaged the baby's throat and vocal chords.

Acids and alkalis can be beneficial when used appropriately. Unfortunately, when used incorrectly or with malicious intent, they can result in great harm and hurt to others and oneself. Hence, care and caution must be taken when handling acids and alkalis.

Chemical Burns

Chemical burns are often caused by skin contact with strong acids and alkalis. Traditionally, a chemical burn is classified by doctors as a first-, second- or third-degree burn. Alternatively, they may be described as superficial burn, partial thickness injury and full thickness injury, respectively.

- **First-degree burn** (superficial burn) refers to injury to the outermost layer of the skin (epidermis).
- **Second-degree burn** (partial thickness injury) refers to injury extending to the second layer of skin (dermis).
- **Third-degree burn** (full thickness injury) refers to injury that has destroyed both the epidermis and the dermis.

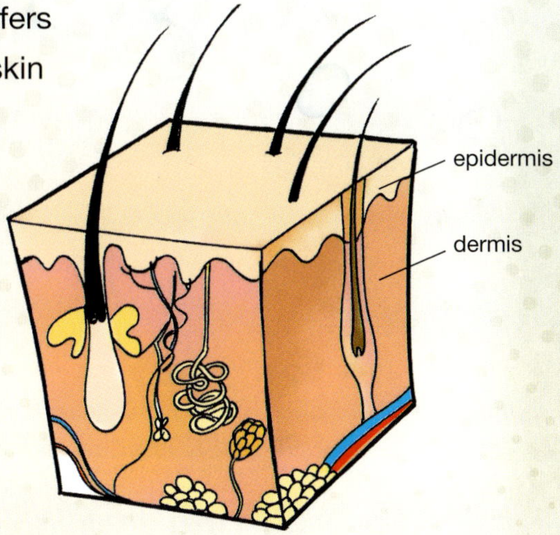

Did You Know?

Which is more dangerous — Acid or Alkali?

Acid burns bring about the denaturation of proteins and produce dry scabs that limit penetration of the acid and prevent further damage. This is known as **coagulation necrosis**.

Alkalis also denature proteins, hydrolyse fats and turn tissues into a liquid mass. In contrast to acid burns, penetration of the alkali is not halted and results in extensive damage. This is known as **liquefaction necrosis**.

Hence, alkali exposure can result in more severe damage compared to acid exposure. Other factors such as pH and concentration of the chemical as well as the contact time will also impact the severity of the burn.

Did You Know?

Cement burn can occur when skin comes into contact with wet cement. This is due to the formation of calcium hydroxide when cement reacts with water and sweat. The rising pH due to the formation of the alkaline hydroxide ions can cause burns to the skin. Workers may be unaware as they will not feel immediate pain when in contact with the wet cement, though damage to the skin may have already occurred.

Use of Acids in Forensic Science – Serial Number Restoration

Acids can cause serious injuries when they come in contact with the skin. However, they can prove useful in uncovering serial numbers that have been obliterated. In cases of car thefts, the perpetrators often try to remove the engine numbers in order to avoid having the stolen cars traced back to their original owners. With the help of acids, such obliterations can be restored.

Stamping

When a serial number is stamped onto a metal surface — such as a car engine or a gun barrel — the metal under each number is placed under permanent stress as compared to the surrounding area.

Obliteration

The number is mechanically removed, usually by smoothing the surface with a metal file. This obliterated number may still be restored when suitable chemicals are applied as the strained areas react differently compared to the surrounding areas.

Restoration

1. Polish the metal surface with a fine abrasive.
2. Apply suitable chemicals to the surface and observe the etching process.
3. Halt the process by flushing with water as soon as the numbers become obvious.
4. Have a camera handy to document the restored serial numbers.

Safety First

Do you recognise these symbols? Can you match them to their meanings?

Gases under pressure

Explosive

Acute toxicity (Severe)

Flammables

Corrosive

When working with chemicals, what are some precautions you should take?

Put on Personal Protective Equipment (PPE)

- Lab coat
- Safety goggles
- Gloves
- Covered shoes

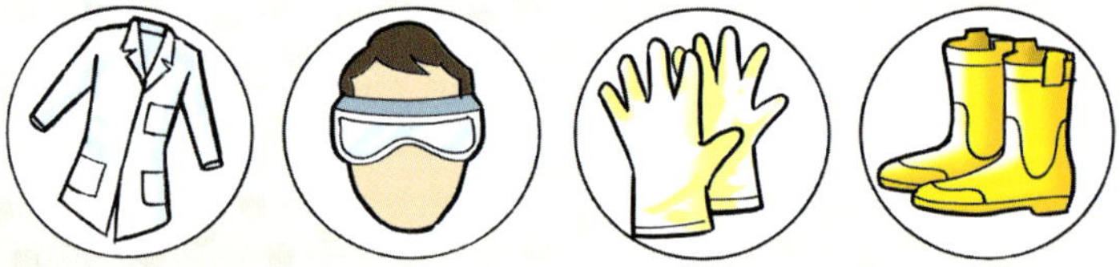

Read the Safety Data Sheet (SDS) supplied with the chemical

A Safety Data Sheet (SDS) is an important safety document that provides information and instructions on the safe use of a particular chemical or material. This document should be kept in an area close to where the chemicals or materials are stored so that they are easily accessible for reference.

There are 16 sections on an SDS. What are some important things you can find?

Here are three important sections from the SDS for acetic acid:

Section 1: Identification of the substance/mixture and of the company/undertaking
Product Name: Acetic Acid Product Number: 460299 CAS-No. 64-19-7

Section 4: First aid measures
Description of first aid measures **If inhaled:** Move person into fresh air. If breathing stops, provide artificial respiration. Consult a physician. **In case of eye contact:** Immediately flush with plenty of water for at least 15 minutes and consult a physician. **In case of skin contact:** Immediately remove contaminated clothing and shoes. Wash off with soap and plenty of water. Consult a physician. **If ingested:** Do not induce vomiting. Never give anything by mouth to an unconscious person. Seek medical attention if symptoms appear.

Section 8: Exposure controls/personal protection
Personal Protective Equipment **Eye/face protection:** Use safety goggles and face shield. **Skin protection:** Wear chemical-resistant gloves, footwear and protective clothing.

Chapter 7

BLOOD, BLOOD EVERYWHERE

Ouch! You have accidentally cut your finger. A red liquid is dripping out of your wound. You know it is blood, but what really is blood?

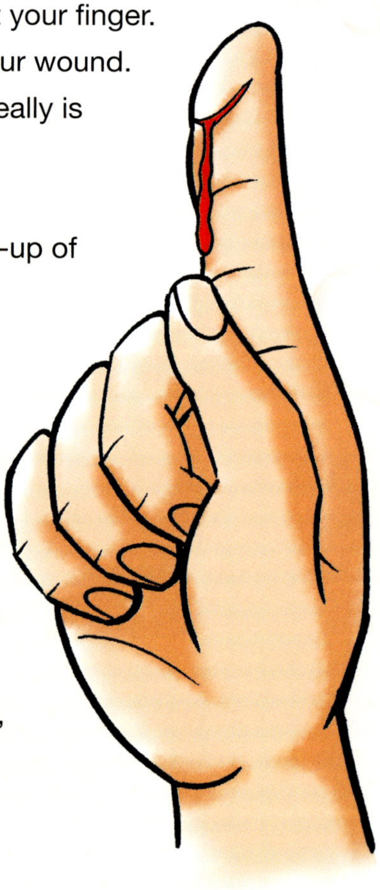

Understanding the overall make-up of blood and its properties assists the forensic scientist to better analyse bloodstain patterns to understand a bloodshed event. Blood is a specialised body fluid that makes up 7% to 8% of our body weight. An average-sized man has about 5-6 litres of blood and a woman, about 4-5 litres.

What is in Our Blood?

Blood is a mixture of two main components. The liquid portion is known as the plasma and constitutes approximately 55% of our whole blood. The solid portion comprising cells, is known as the formed elements and constitutes the other 45%.

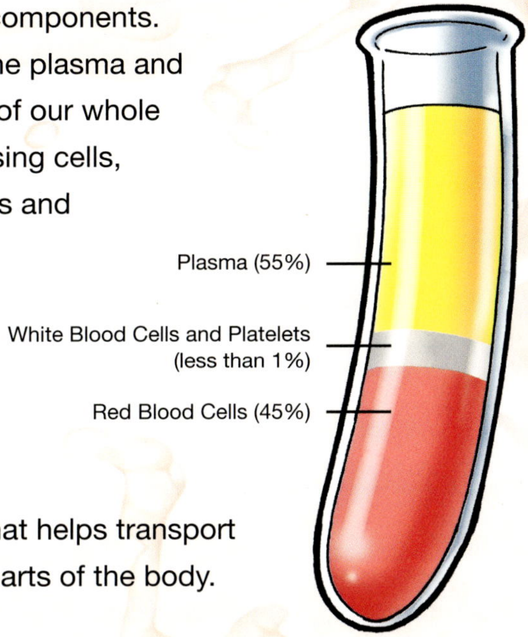

Plasma is a light yellow liquid that helps transport nutrients and proteins to other parts of the body.

Red blood cells contain the protein haemoglobin, which combines with oxygen (O_2) in the lungs to form oxyhaemoglobin and helps transport oxygen to the tissues. Besides binding to oxygen, haemoglobin can also be easily bound to carbon monoxide. In cases of carbon monoxide poisoning, the victim experiences a lack of oxygen and dies with the characteristic cherry red coloration in the lips and face. In cases where carbon monoxide poisoning is suspected, a sample of the victim's or deceased's blood is taken and examined by toxicologists for the presence of carboxyhaemoglobin.

White blood cells play a huge role in defending the body against infections.

Did You Know?

From 1911 to the 1980s, coal miners often brought canaries underground as companions because these birds could detect carbon monoxide, an odourless and colourless toxic gas that may be present in mines. These sentinels* were more sensitive to toxic gases and would show signs of distress and become sick before the miners, thus serving as a means to warn the miners to evacuate to safety. This decades-old practice has since been replaced by technological improvements. These days, portable handheld detectors are used instead to test the air quality in mines. The poor canaries are thus spared!

Human blood is red in colour, but its shade ranges from vivid red to very dark red. The colour depends on whether the blood contains the bright red oxyhaemoglobin (haemoglobin that is bound to oxygen) or the dark or bluish-red deoxyhaemoglobin (haemoglobin without oxygen present).

---

* Sentinel animal: An animal placed in an environment to detect or monitor the presence of a harmful substance.

Is blood always red?

Human blood is red due to the presence of **haemoglobin**. Not all animal species have blood that is red. Blood can be green, blue or even purple!

Spiders and crustaceans have blue blood because of the protein known as **haemocyanin**.

Leeches have green blood due to the protein **chlorocruorin** that is present.

Some marine worms use the blood protein **hemerythrin** to transport oxygen which turns their blood a purple colour.

ABO Blood Group System

There are four blood types, A, B, O and AB. The presence or absence of A and B antigens on the surfaces of red blood cells determines a person's blood type.

Type A: Presence of the A antigen on red blood cells
Type B: Presence of the B antigen on red blood cells
Type AB: Presence of both A and B antigens on red blood cells
Type O: Absence of both A and B antigens on red blood cells

What are antigens and antibodies, and how do they relate to blood type?

An antigen is a substance that causes your immune system to produce antibodies against it.

An antibody is a protein created by your body to fight against foreign substances known as antigens.

An **antigen-antibody interaction** works like a lock-and-key mechanism. The antibody binds to a specific antigen, just as how a particular key fits a particular lock.

Antigens

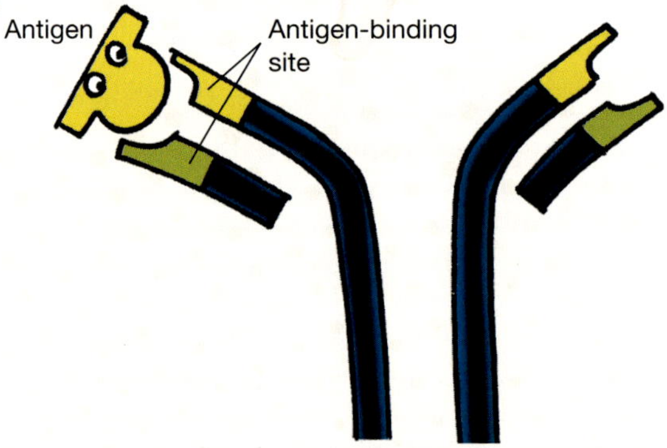

Antibody

ABO Blood Group System				
Group	A	B	AB	O
Red Blood Cell Type	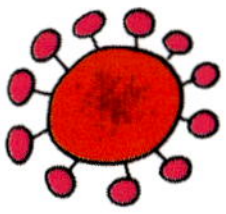			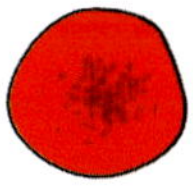
Antigens Present	 Antigens A	 Antigens B	 Antigens A & B	None
Antibodies Present	 Anti-B	 Anti-A	None	 Anti-A & Anti-B

In a transfusion, if a person with type A blood were to be given type B blood, it would result in the clumping or agglutination of blood, which can lead to death. This is because type A blood would have the A antigen and anti-B antibodies, which interact with the B-antigen present in type B blood.

In the past, forensic scientists used to perform serological tests on bloodstains left at scenes, in order to determine the blood type. This assisted them in eliminating a suspect if his/her blood group was different from that found at the scene.

Today, DNA analysis has largely taken over the role of serology as it provides more comprehensive and specific results on unknown bloodstains. From a bloodstain, scientists can now identify the individual instead of only being able to tell his blood group.

- **Can a person with type O blood get a blood transfusion from a person with type AB blood? Why?**
- **Besides identifying the blood type, what other information can be derived from blood that allows for identification?**

At the Crime Scene

What are those reddish-brown stains on the kitchen floor? Could the stains be blood? Are they human blood or animal blood?

1. Is it blood?

A. Luminol Test

Remember watching CSI and seeing investigators spray the walls of a crime scene to reveal glowing blue spots in a darkened room? Well, that is luminol in action!

Luminol reacts with the iron in blood to produce a faint glow (chemiluminescence) that lasts for about 30 seconds — a short period of time, but sufficient for the investigators to observe and document the result. Luminol can detect traces of blood even if they have been cleaned away. It is very difficult to get rid of bloodstains totally!

B. Kastle-Meyer Test

A Kastle-Meyer colour test is often used to screen for blood. It involves the use of a chemical known as phenolphthalein. The reduced form of phenolphthalein is colourless and will react with hydrogen peroxide and the haemoglobin in blood to produce a pink coloration.

Can other substances react and produce a pink colour? Yes. This is because the Kastle-Meyer test is not a specific test for blood. Vegetables such as potatoes and horseradish can also result in a pink colouration, as can oxidants such as copper and nickel salts.

Is the luminol test specific?

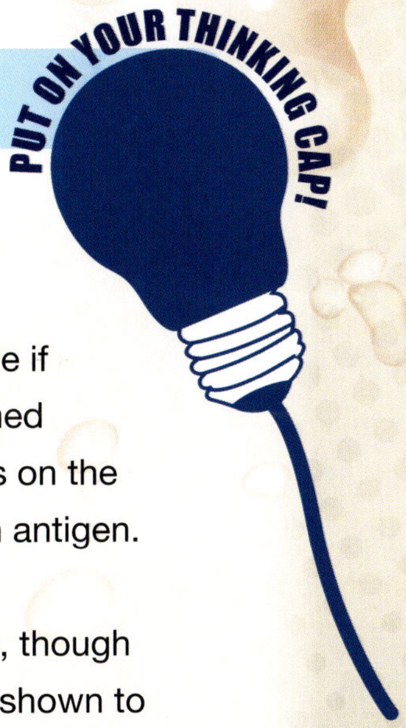

2. Is the blood of human or animal origin?

A test known as **Hexagon OBTI** is a quick test to determine if a bloodstain is of human origin. This test is usually performed after an initial Kastle-Meyer screening test is done. It works on the principles of immunology where an antibody reacts with an antigen.

The Hexagon OBTI test is specific for human and primates, though the blood of rabbits, weasels and badgers have also been shown to react positively to the test. However, in most cases, primates, rabbits, badgers and weasels can be excluded from the crime scene and the bloodstain is concluded to be of human origin.

Bloodstains

Anatomy of a stain

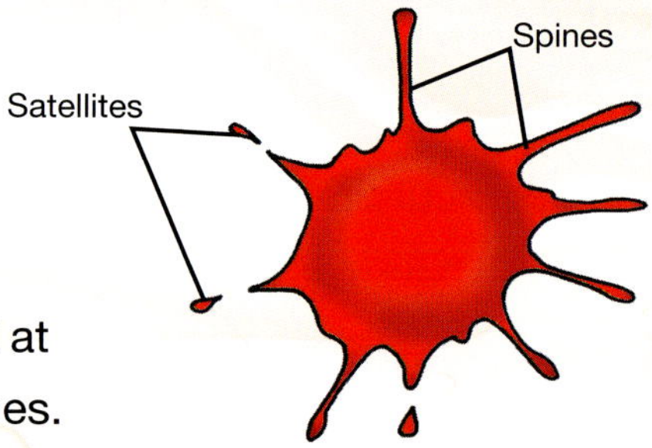

Bloodstains are often encountered at crime scenes, especially violent ones. The analysis of these bloodstain patterns, coupled with other forensic findings such as those from autopsy, DNA, marks and prints, and trace evidence, help to reconstruct the who, what, when, where, why and how of a crime.

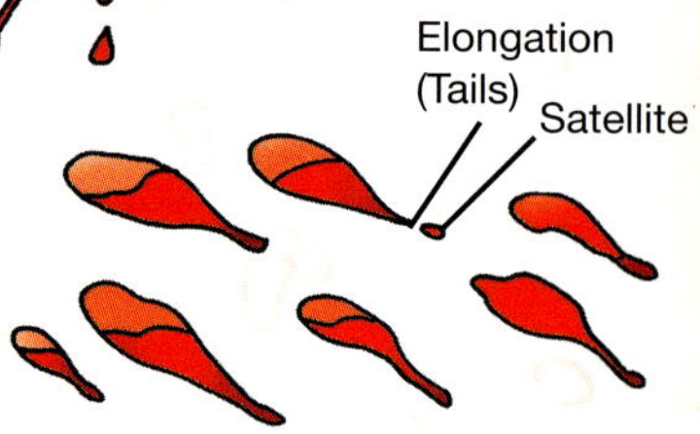

Examples of bloodstain patterns encountered at crime scenes

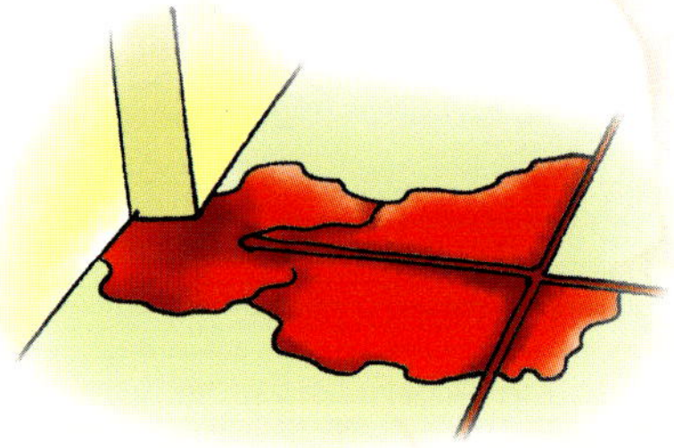

Accumulation of blood at one spot

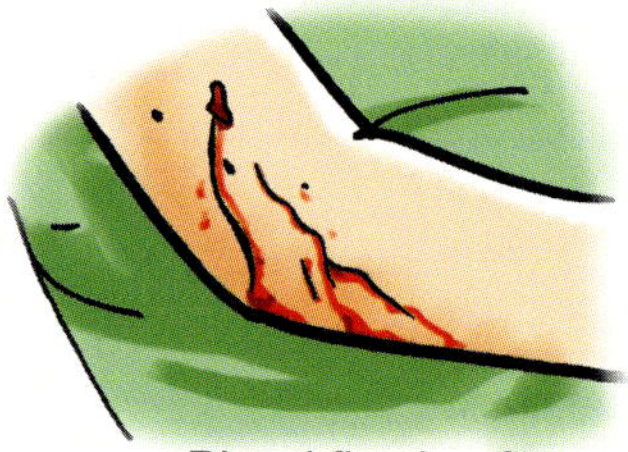

Blood flowing from a wound

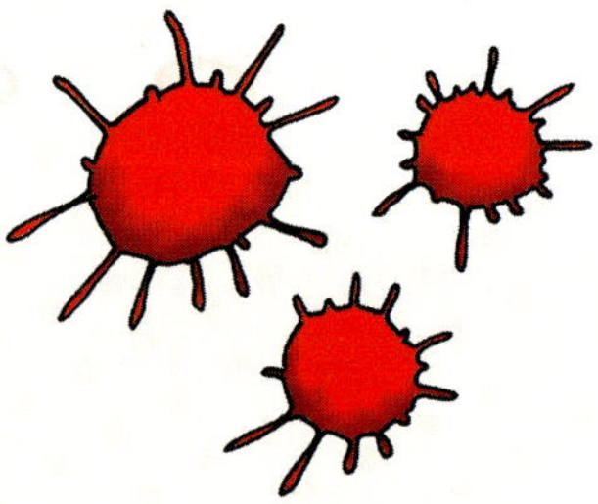

Blood droplets from a wound or an object

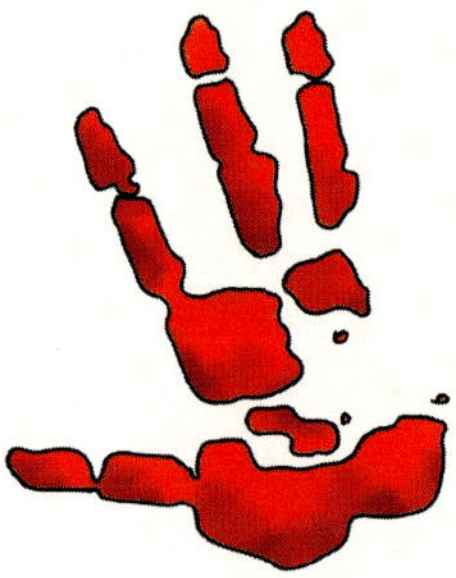

Bloody imprints

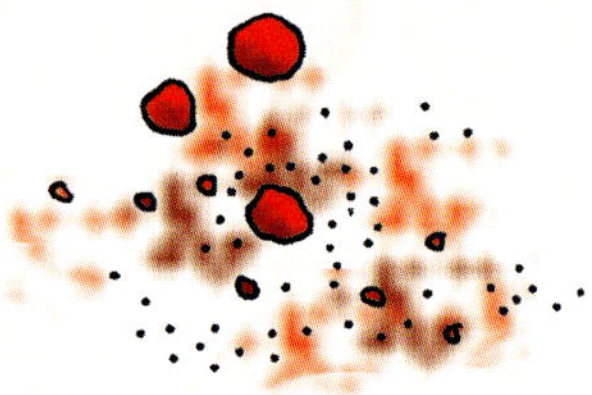

Bloodstains resulting from a gunshot

Did You Know?

In the event of a breached artery, blood spurts out, similar to a small cut on a water hose under pressure. Fluctuations of the arterial blood can sometimes be observed. Each fluctuation is due to differences in blood pressure as the heart pumps.

Impact Angles

The shape of bloodstains can provide clues to the angle at which the blood drops hit a surface. The more perpendicular the angle at which the blood drop strikes the target surface, the more circular the bloodstain. As the angle of impact becomes more acute (smaller), the shape of the bloodstain becomes more elliptical.

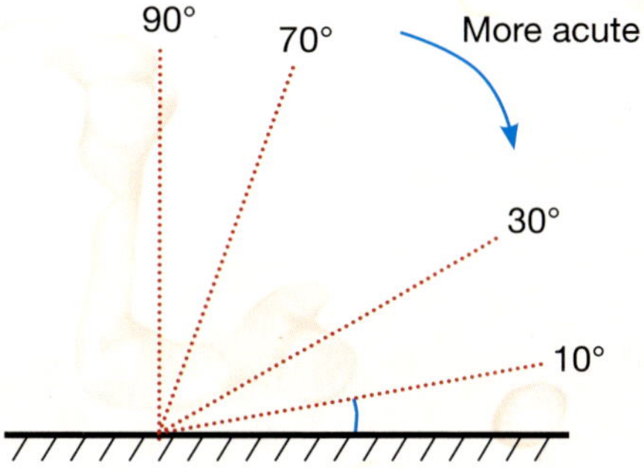

ANGLE OF IMPACT

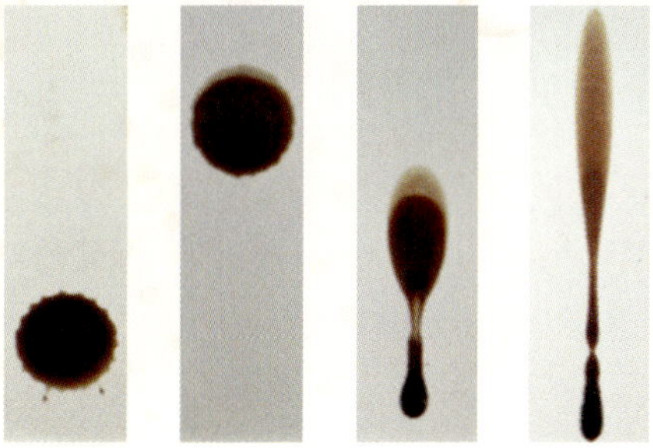

90° 70° 30° 10°

How can you use trigonometry to calculate impact angle?

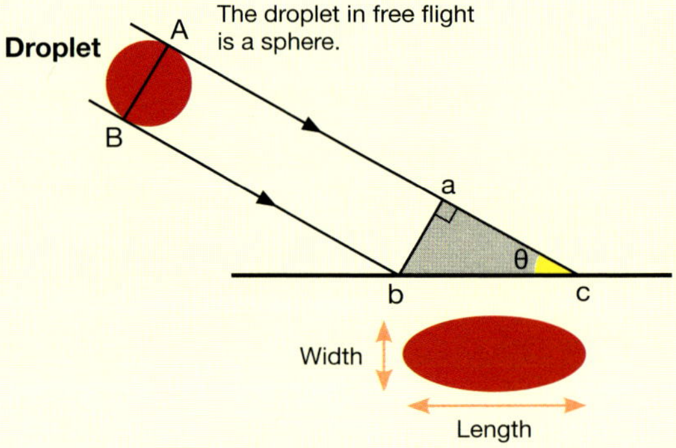

$$\sin\theta = \frac{\text{opposite}}{\text{hypotenuse}}$$

$$= \frac{\text{width}}{\text{length}}$$

$$\theta = \sin^{-1}\frac{\text{width}}{\text{length}}$$

Example:

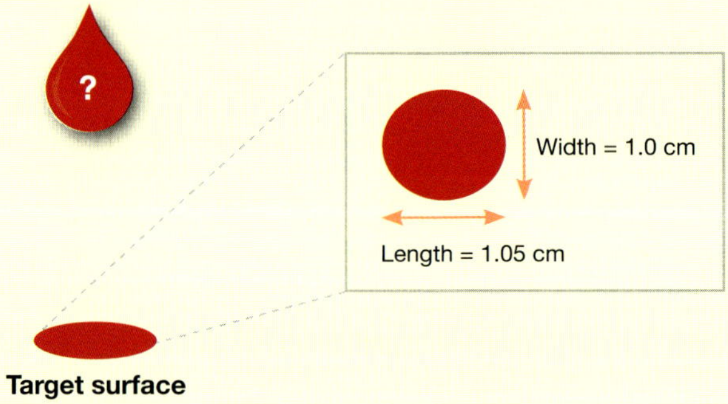

$$\sin\theta = \frac{\text{width}}{\text{length}}$$

$$= \frac{1.0\text{ cm}}{1.05\text{ cm}}$$

$$= 0.95$$

$$\theta = \sin^{-1}0.95$$

$$= 71.8°$$

Level Up! -- What's My Angle?

Determining the Impact Angle

Step 1: Outline the stain, excluding the tail end to get a symmetrical oval shape.

Step 2: Measure the length and wide of the oval.

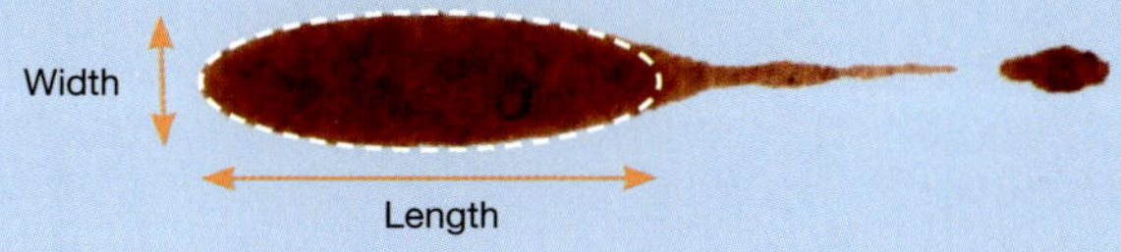

Length = ____ cm

Width = ____ cm

$\sin\theta = \dfrac{\text{width}}{\text{length}}$

$= \dfrac{\_\_\_\_\ \text{cm}}{\_\_\_\_\ \text{cm}}$

$= \_\_\_\_$

$\theta = \sin^{-1} \_\_\_\_$

$= \_\_\_\_^{\circ}$

From the Vaults – Stories from Singapore's Past

Yishun Triple Murder

In September 2008, police were called to investigate a fall from height, involving a woman, at Block 349, Yishun Avenue 11. In order to determine where the woman had fallen from, the police started checking all units. They caught sight of some bloodstains on the padlock of a unit and knocked on the door. A man named Wang opened the door and told the police that he had gone on a killing spree. When the police entered the flat, they were shocked to find two other persons lying dead while another victim was barely clinging on to life.

Persons Involved

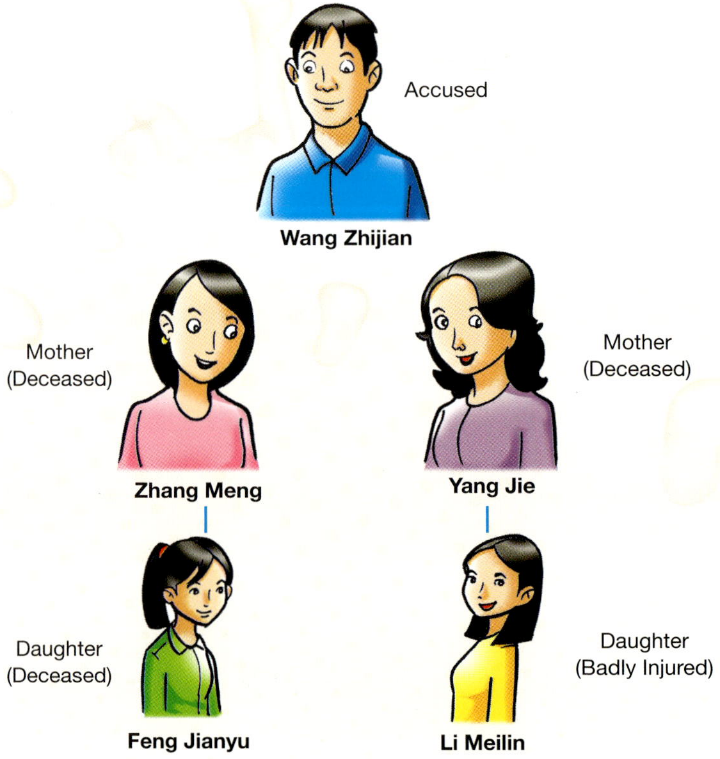

Wang Zhijian, Zhang Meng, Feng Jianyu

- Zhang Meng and her daughter Feng Jianyu rented two bedrooms in the Yishun flat.
- Wang Zhijian, who was on a social visit pass in Singapore, had begun a relationship with Zhang Meng back when they were in China.
- In his statement, Wang recounted how Zhang Meng would not allow him to leave the bedroom when the others were in the flat, and that he was also not allowed to interact with them.

Yang Jie and Li Meilin

- Yang Jie and her daughter Li Meilin were tenants of the remaining bedroom in the house.
- They were not related to Wang Zhijian, Zhang Meng or Feng Jianyu.

Trigger

The tragedy was sparked off by Zhang Meng's demand for money from Wang Zhijian to buy crabs for dinner. Wang was reluctant to do so as he felt it was a waste of money. Moreover, they had just eaten crabs a week ago. Zhang became angry and started scolding Wang with vulgarities and humiliating him.

Ensuing events

After their argument, Zhang went to sleep. As Wang lay down on his mattress in the same room, his mind kept wandering to past occasions when he had been physically and verbally abused by Zhang and her daughter. Unable to fall asleep, he got up and went into the kitchen to "have some air". It was there that he grabbed a knife and headed back to his bedroom.

What the police saw in the flat

There were bloodstains in every corner of the flat. The bodies of Zhang and her daughter lay motionless in Zhang's room. Autopsy results identified 48 knife wounds on Zhang's body and 45 knife wounds on Feng's body. Li Meilin was barely alive and lying at one corner of the bathroom in the kitchen.

What happened?

What events transpired at the scene? How did Feng Jianyu end up dead in her mother's room? How did Yang Jie fall from the kitchen window and what happened to Li Meilin? What role did Wang play in the death of the three deceased persons, and the near-death state of Li Meilin? Bloodstain pattern analysis and scene reconstruction provided vital answers to the court on the sequence of events, and assisted in the administration of justice.

Reconstruction Findings

The judge accorded "much weight to Li's testimony, because Li was the sole survivor and could give direct evidence, and her evidence was independently corroborated by the forensic evidence and major points in the Reconstruction Report".

Attack of Zhang Meng and Feng Jianyu

After grabbing the knife and heading back to the room, Wang moved to where Zhang was sleeping and stabbed her repeatedly in the abdomen. As the stabbing went on, the door to the bedroom opened and Feng Jianyu, Zhang's daughter, appeared at the doorway. Wang proceeded to attack and stab her repeatedly in the abdomen until she collapsed. Wang subsequently left the room.

Attack of Yang Jie and Li Meilin

Both Yang Jie and Li Meilin were sleeping in their room when Meilin was awakened by the sound of heavy breathing outside their room. The door then swung open and Wang rushed in, slashing her on her cheek. Realising that Yang Jie had already run out of the bedroom, Wang then left the bedroom to pursue her. In a bid to escape, Yang Jie had climbed out of the kitchen window and was holding on to the laundry pole holders below the window sill. Upon finding Yang Jie, Wang Zhijian used a chopper to cut her fingers, causing her to lose her grip and fall to her death.

Wang went back to the bedroom and continued to attack Li Meilin. She managed to escape to the kitchen and locked herself in the kitchen bathroom. Unfortunately, Wang tore down the door and continued to attack her with a knife until she was motionless on the bathroom floor.

Verdict

Although Wang repeatedly denied having anything to do with Yang Jie's death, the forensic evidence showed otherwise. Wang was eventually found guilty of the triple murders of Zhang Meng, Feng Jianyu and Yang Jie and sentenced to death.

Chapter 8

FORENSIC SCANDALS

Scientific fraud is rare. However, there have been several instances where forensic scientists engaged in actions that violated the ethical code of conduct and jeopardised the administration of justice.

One notorious case was that of Joyce Gilchrist, who was a highly regarded forensic scientist with the Oklahoma City Police Department.

Joyce Gilchrist: Black Magic or Bad Science?

Joyce Gilchrist was a forensic examiner for 21 years in the Oklahoma City Police Department. During her time there, she was nicknamed "Black Magic" for her uncanny talent at matching DNA evidence. Not only did she examine evidence from over 3,000 criminal cases, she was also a star witness in several cases.

In 1994, she was promoted from forensic chemist to the role of supervisor after just nine years on the job. However, her colleagues began to raise concerns about her work and there were suspicions that Gilchrist had put people in prison more with sorcery than with science — she seemed to be able to do things with evidence that no one else could!

An investigation into these allegations was launched and among the many findings, her lab notes were found to be incomplete or inadequate. She was eventually fired in September 2001 after being accused of flawed analyses and providing false or misleading testimony in criminal cases.

It was found that her evidence had led in part to 23 people being sentenced to death. At the time of her dismissal, 12 of these 23 people had already been executed. One of the surviving victims of her fraudulent work was Jeffrey Todd Pierce, who was wrongfully convicted of rape in 1986 despite having both no criminal record and a good alibi. Gilchrist claimed that his hair samples were "microscopically consistent" with the hairs found at the crime scene. After spending 15 years behind bars, Pierce was exonerated in 2001 following a re-examination using DNA evidence.

What Do Ethics and Integrity Mean?

Ethics and integrity often go hand in hand. **Ethics** refers to a person's moral principles that help him distinguish between right and wrong. **Integrity** is the belief and courage to do the right thing regardless of the circumstances and consequences. It is very important for forensic scientists to possess both ethics and integrity and ensure that all analyses are carried out in an objective, complete and fair manner.

A forensic scientist's unethical actions or flawed analyses may not only allow guilty persons to get away scot-free, but also cause innocent persons to be wrongfully convicted and imprisoned. In the case of Joyce Gilchrist, her flawed analyses and false testimonies were fuelled by her hunger for fame and recognition. Because of that, more than 1,700 cases in which Gilchrist's evidence was significant for conviction came into doubt. These cases had to be re-opened and revisited, which was draining on both time and resources. Her wrongdoings had also caused anguish to the parties involved, especially those who had been wrongfully put behind bars.

It is also important that a forensic scientist remains unbiased at all times. The overriding duty of the forensic scientist is to uphold truth and justice, and not be partial to the party that hired him. One must not produce a favourable result or report because the party hiring is paying a huge sum of money, or because one feels that the accused should be convicted for the crime committed.

A forensic scientist must also be aware of the strengths and limitations of each test employed, the evidential value of the results obtained, and the range of conclusions he can reach. Any slight error on the part of the forensic scientist can have far-ranging consequences — not just for the persons involved but also for their families, the public and the judicial system.

> "If the law has made you a witness, remain a man of science. You have no victim to avenge, no guilty or innocent person to convict or save — you must bear testimony within the limits of science."

Dr P.C.H. Brouardel
19th-century medico-legalist

From the Vaults: The Birmingham Six

On 21 November 1974, two bombs exploded in Birmingham, England. The explosive devices had been placed in two pubs in central Birmingham — the Mulberry Bush at the foot of the Rotunda, and the Tavern in the Town on New Street. A third bomb had been planted outside a bank on Hagley Road but failed to detonate.

As a result of the explosions, 21 people were killed and 162 were wounded. Until the London bombings on 7 July 2005, this was the most injurious and serious attack in the country since World War II. Following the incident, several people were detained.

The suspects later became known as the "Birmingham Six". They were interrogated extensively without any breaks, food or sleep. Eventually, several of them signed confessions.

In the trial of the Birmingham Six in June 1975, the jury found all six men guilty and sentenced them to life imprisonment. It was only after being wrongfully imprisoned for more than 16 years that the six men were exonerated.

What Went Wrong?

In the investigations during the original trial, Dr Frank Skuse, a forensic chemist, had used a chemical test known as the Griess Test on the six suspects. Two suspects, Hill and Power, tested positive.

The Griess test is a **screening/presumptive test** for the presence of nitroglycerine, a compound commonly found in explosives. It is not a specific test to identify the substance, i.e. other substances may also test positive when subjected to the same test. Further **confirmatory tests** should have been done to determine the actual presence or identity of the substance. At the trial, Dr Skuse stated that he was "99 per cent certain" that Hill and Power had handled explosives, based on the results of the Greiss Test.

As a result, based on scientific conclusions that were flawed and confessions that could have been extracted under torture, six innocent men were put behind bars.

Freeing the Innocent from Wrongful Convictions

The Innocence Project is a non-profit organisation that works to exonerate those who have been wrongfully convicted. It advocates for reforms in the criminal justice system to prevent injustice from recurring. It also helps the exonerated rebuild their lives and assimilate back into society. The organisation was founded in 1992 in USA by two American lawyers, Peter Neufeld and Barry Scheck.

With the same overarching vision, others have joined the Innocence Network, including organisations in the Netherlands, Ireland, New Zealand, Argentina, Taiwan, Italy, Israel, Canada and Australia.

The Innocence Project (Singapore) is an organisation led by law students from the National University of Singapore. Together with the Pro Bono Services Office of the Law Society of Singapore and the Association of Criminal Lawyers of Singapore, the organisation seeks to help those who believe they have been wrongfully incarcerated.

INNOCENCE PROJECT SINGAPORE

הסניגוריה הציבורית
Public Defense

冤獄平反協會
TAIWAN ASSOCIATION FOR INNOCENCE

Innocence Canada

INNOCENCE PROJECT ARGENTINA

IRISH INNOCENCE PROJECT
Tionscadal Neamhchiontachta na hÉireann

What Would You Do?

Scenario 1

You were assigned to test five pieces of evidence recovered from a crime scene. Results from the first four pieces of evidence all point towards one suspect. Processing the last piece of evidence would require another two weeks.

On hearing this update, the investigator is keen to press charges against the suspect and requests that you quickly move on to write the report based on the four pieces of evidence, and "forget about the last piece of evidence as it would just be a waste of time". What would you do?

Scenario 2

You noticed that a senior scientist working on a big case involving 100 samples was using an expired chemical for the analysis he was conducting. You later tested the expired chemical and found that it did not respond well to the usual tests.

You inform the senior of the testing, but he tells you that the court is expecting the case report in a week's time and there is insufficient time to repeat all the analyses with a new batch of the chemical. What would you do?

Whenever an ethical dilemma is encountered, it is useful for the forensic scientist to pause and consider the situation. Discuss with co-workers: Is it legal or morally correct? Are there other means to resolve the situation?

Guiding Questions

- What are some of the actions that you would take?
- What are some of the possible consequences of these actions?
- If you choose not to take any action, what would be some of the consequences?

TAKING THE NEXT STEP

Congratulations! You have completed this leg of your journey in discovering the fascinating world of forensic science. Has your interest been piqued? Have you gained a better understanding of the different forensic disciplines? Well, we hope you have!

Learning is an ongoing process and does not just stop at the end of the book. Take the time to go through the chapters again, try answering the questions that are posed in each chapter and participate in some of the Level Up! activities — we look forward to receiving your handwritten passages in our mail!

Thank you for accompanying us on this wonderful learning journey. Check out our website or Facebook page to find out more about the work we do and the activities we provide!

— The Forensic Experts Group